拥抱自然 思考社会 回归常识 丰盈自我

影响人类的伟大思想

企鹅人文经典

W0356365

论语选萃

The First Ten Books

英汉对照

［春秋］孔 丘 著

刘殿爵 英译

付雅丽 白话文翻译、注释

中国出版集团公司

中国对外翻译出版有限公司

图书在版编目(CIP)数据

论语选萃：英汉对照/(春秋) 孔丘著；刘殿爵英译；付雅丽译、注.
—北京：中国对外翻译出版有限公司，2011.12
(企鹅人文经典)
ISBN 978-7-5001-2880-9

Ⅰ.①论… Ⅱ.①孔…②刘…③付… Ⅲ.①英语–汉语–对照读物
②儒家 Ⅳ.①H319.4: B

中国版本图书馆CIP数据核字(2011)第234724号

(著作权合同登记：图字 01-2009-5520 号)

www.penguin.com.cn
The Analects first published in Penguin Classics 1979
This extract published in Penguin Books 2005

Taken from the Penguin Classics edition of *The Analects*,
translated and introduced by D. C. Lau
Set by Rowland Phototypesetting Ltd, Bury St Edmunds, Suffolk

出版发行 / 中国对外翻译出版有限公司
地　　址 / 北京市西城区车公庄大街甲4号物华大厦6层
电　　话 / (010) 68359376　68359303　68359719
邮　　编 / 100044
传　　真 / (010) 68357870
电子邮箱 / book@ctpc.com.cn
网　　址 / http://www.ctpc.com.cn

总 经 理 / 林国夫
出版策划 / 张高里
项目负责 / 徐　静
责任编辑 / 徐　静

封面设计 / 奇文堂·潘峰
排　　版 / 竹页图文
印　　刷 / 北京建泰印刷有限公司
经　　销 / 新华书店北京发行所

规　　格 / 630×920毫米　1/16
印　　张 / 13
版　　次 / 2012年3月第一版
印　　次 / 2012年3月第一次

ISBN 978-7-5001-2880-9　**定价：16.00元**

中国对外翻译出版有限公司与企鹅图书有限公司联合出版

观　念

——《伟大的思想》代序

每隔一段时间，媒体就喜欢评选一次“影响世界的 X 个人”或者“改变历史的 X 项发明”。然而，在我看来，几乎所有人类史上最重大的变革，首先都是一种观念的变革。

我们今天之所以会关注气候的变暖与生物多样性的保存，是因为我们看待地球的方式变了，我们比以前更加意识到人在自然中的位置，也更加了解自然其实是一个动态的系统。放弃了人类可以主宰地球的世界观，这就意味着我们接受了一个观念的变化。同样地，我们不再相信男人一出生就该主宰女人，甚至也不再认为男女之别是不可动摇的本质区分，这也是观念的变化。如果说环保运动和女权运动有任何影响的话，那些影响一定就是从大脑开始的。也不要只看好事，20 世纪最惨绝人寰的浩劫最初也只不过是一些小小的观念，危险的观念。比如说一位德国人，他相信人类的进化必以“次等种族”的灭绝为代价……

这套丛书不叫“伟大的巨著”，是因为它们体积都不大，而且还有不少是抽取自某些名著的章节。

可它们却全是伟大的观念，例如达尔文的论天择，潘恩的论常识，它们共同构成了人类的观念地图。从头看它们一遍，就是检视文明所走过的道路，从深处理解我们今天变成这个样子的原因。

也许你会发现其中有些陌生的名字，或者看起来没有那么“伟大”的篇章（譬如普鲁斯特追忆他的阅读时光），但你千万不要小看它们。因为真正重要、真正能够产生启蒙效果的观念往往具有跨界移动的能力，它会跨越时空，离开它原属的领域，在另一个世界产生意外的效果。就像马可·波罗在监狱里述说的异国图景，当时有谁料得到那些荒诞的故事会诱发出哥伦布的旅程呢？我也无法猜测，这套小书的读者里头会不会有下一个哥伦布，他将带着令人惊奇的观念航向自己的大海。

梁文道

《伟大的思想》中文版序

企鹅《伟大的思想》丛书于2004年开始出版。在英国，至今已付印80种，尚有20种计划出版。美国出版的丛书规模略小，德国的同类丛书规模更小一些。丛书销量已远远超过200万册，在全球很多人中间，尤其是学生当中，普及了哲学和政治学。中文版《伟大的思想》丛书的推出，迈出了新的一步，令人欢欣鼓舞。

推出这套丛书的目的是让读者再次与一些伟大的非小说类经典著作面对面地交流。太长时间以来，确定版本依据这样一个假设——读者在教室里学习这些著作，因此需要导读、详尽的注释、参考书目等。此类版本无疑非常有用，但我想，如果能够重建托马斯•潘恩《常识》或约翰•罗斯金《艺术与人生》初版时的环境，重新营造更具亲和力的氛围，那也是一件有意思的事。当时，读者除了原作者及其自身的理性思考外，没有其他参照。

这样做有一定的缺点：每个作者的话难免有难解或不可解之处，一些重要的背景知识会缺失。例如，读者对亨利•梭罗创作时的情况毫无头绪，也不了解该书得到的认可及其影响。不过这样做的优点也很明显。最突出的优点是，作者的初衷又一次变得重要起来——托马斯•潘恩的愤怒、查尔斯•达尔文的灵光、塞内加的隐逸。这些作家在那么多国家影响了那么多人的生活，其影响不可估量，有的长达几个世纪，读他们书的乐趣罕有匹敌。没有亚当·斯密或阿图尔·叔本华，难以想象我们今天的世界。这些小书的创作年代已很久远，但其中的语言已彻底改变了我们的政治学、经济学、智力生活、社会规划和宗教信仰。

《伟大的思想》丛书一直求新求变。地区不同，收录的作家也不同。在中国或美国，一些作家更受欢迎。英国《伟大的思想》收录的一些作家在其他地方则默默无闻。称其为“伟大的思想”，我们亦慎之又慎。思想之伟大，在于其影响之深远，而不意味着这些思想是“好”的，实际上一些书可列入“坏思想”之列。丛书中很多作家受到同一丛书其他作家的很大影响，例如，马塞尔·普鲁斯特承认受约翰·罗斯金影响很大，米歇尔·德·蒙田也承认深受塞内加影响，但其他有些作家彼此憎恨，如果发现他们被收入同一丛书，一定会气愤难平。不过，读者可自行决定这些思想是否合理。我们衷心希望，您能在阅读这些杰作中得到乐趣。

《伟大的思想》出版者

西蒙·温德尔

Introduction to the Chinese Editions of Great Ideas

Penguin's Great Ideas series began publication in 2004. In the UK we now have 80 copies in print with plans to publish a further 20. A somewhat smaller list is published in the USA and a related, even smaller series in Germany. The books have sold now well over two million copies and have popularized philosophy and politics for many people around the world — particularly students. The launch of a Chinese Great Ideas series is an extremely exciting new development.

The intention behind the series was to allow readers to be once more face to face with some of the great non-fiction classics. For too long the editions of these books were created on the assumption that you were studying them in the classroom and that the student needed an introduction, extensive notes, a bibliography and so on. While this sort of edition is of course extremely useful, I thought it would be interesting to recreate a more intimate feeling — to recreate the atmosphere in which, for example, Thomas Paine's *Common Sense* or John Ruskin's *On Art and Life* was first published — where the reader has no other guide than the original author and his or her own common sense.

This method has its severe disadvantages — there will inevitably be statements made by each author which are either hard or impossible to understand, some important context might be missing. For example the reader has no clue as to the conditions under which Henry Thoreau was writing his book and the reader cannot be aware of the book's reception or influence. The advantages however are very clear—most importantly the original intentions of the author become once more important. The sense of anger in Thomas Paine, of intellectual excitement in Charles Darwin, of resignation in Seneca—few things can be more thrilling than to read writers who have had such immeasurable influence on so many lives, sometimes for centuries, in many different countries. Our world would not make sense without Adam Smith or Arthur Schopenhauer—our politics, economics, intellectual lives, social planning, religious beliefs have all been fundamentally changed by the words in these little books, first written down long ago.

The Great Ideas series continues to change and evolve. In different parts of the world different writers would be included. In China or in the United States there are some writers who are liked much more than others. In the UK there are writers in the Great Ideas series who are ignored elsewhere. We have also been very careful to call the series Great Ideas—these ideas are great because they have been so enormously influential, but this does not mean that they are Good Ideas—indeed some of the books would probably qualify as Bad Ideas. Many of the writers in the series have been massively influenced by others in the series—for example Marcel Proust owned so much to John Ruskin, Michel de Montaigne to Seneca. But others hated each other and would be distressed to find themselves together in the same series! But readers can decide the validity of these ideas for themselves. We very much hope that you enjoy these remarkable books.

Simon Winder
Publisher
Great Ideas

CONTENTS
目　录

论语选萃

The First Ten Books

Book I

1. ***The Master***[1] said, 'Is it not a pleasure, having learned something, to try it out at ***due***[2] ***intervals***[3]? Is it not a joy to have friends come ***from afar***[4]? Is it not gentlemanly not to take ***offence***[5] when others fail to appreciate your abilities?'

卷 一

Notes

1 the Master 大师，此处指孔子。

2 due [dju:] *a.* 到期的，合适的

3 interval [ˈintəvəl] *n.* 间隔

4 from afar 从远方

5 offence [əˈfens] *n.* 冒犯，触怒

1. 子曰：“学而时习①之，不亦说②乎？有朋自远方来，不亦乐乎？人不知③，而不愠④，不亦君子乎？”

孔子说：“将学到的东西不断地用于实践，不是一件很开心的事吗？有志同道合的朋友从远方来看望自己，难道不会很快乐吗？自己的学识、抱负没有人认可或知道而不心存怨恨，这难道不是君子吗？”

---

① 习：可指温习和实习。

② 说：同“悦”。

③ 人不知：“知”字无宾语，可能是不懂道理，也可能是不了解自己。从下一句“而不愠”来看，后一解释更合适一些。

④ 愠：音 yùn，怨恨。

2. ***Yu Tzu***[1] said, 'It is rare for a man whose character is such that he is good as a son and ***obedient***[2] as a young man to have the ***inclination***[3] to ***transgress***[4] against his superiors; it is unheard of for one who has no such inclination to be inclined to start a ***rebellion***[5]. The gentleman devotes his efforts to the roots, for once the roots are established, the Way will grow ***therefrom***[6]. Being good as a son and obedient as a young man is, perhaps, the root of a man's character.'

Notes

1 Yu Tzu 有子，孔子的学生

2 obedient [ə'bi:djənt] *a.* 顺从的

3 inclination [,inklə'neiʃən] *n.* 倾向

4 transgress [træns'gres] *v.* 违反，侵犯

5 rebellion [ri'beliən] *n.* 作乱，造反

6 therefrom [ðεə'frɔm] *ad.* 从此

2. 有子① 曰："其为人也孝弟②，而好犯上者③，鲜④ 矣；不好犯上，而好作乱者，未之有也⑤。君子务本⑥，本立而道生⑦。孝弟也者，其为仁之本与⑧？"

有子说："一个人很孝顺父母而且疼爱自己的兄弟姐妹，却又经常对别的长辈或地位比自己高的人不恭敬，这样的人是很少的；不会对比自己年长的人或地位高的人不恭，却又经常胡作非为的人我从来没有见过。君子专心致力于根本的事务，基础建立了，治国做人的原则也就有了。孝顺父母、敬爱兄长，这就是仁的根本啊！"

---

① 有子：孔子的学生，姓有，名若，比孔子小 13 岁，一说小 33 岁。后一说较为可信。在《论语》书中，记载的孔子学生，一般都称字，只有曾参和有若称"子"。因此，许多人认为《论语》即由曾参和有若所著述。

② 孝弟：孝，奴隶社会时期所认为的子女对待父母的正确态度；弟，读音和意义与"悌"（音 tì）相同，即弟弟对待兄长的正确态度。旧注说：善事父母曰孝，善事兄长曰弟。

③ 犯上：犯，冒犯、干犯。上，指在上位的人。

④ 鲜：音 xiǎn，少的意思。

⑤ 未之有也：此为"未有之也"的倒装句型。

⑥ 务本：务，专心、致力于。本，根本。

⑦ 道：在中国古代思想里，道有多种含义。此处的道，指孔子提倡的仁道，即以仁为核心的整个道德思想体系及其在实际生活的体现。简单讲，就是治国做人的基本原则。

⑧ 为仁之本：仁是孔子哲学思想的最高范畴，又是伦理道德准则。为仁之本，即以孝悌作为仁的根本。还有一种解释，认为古代的"仁"就是"人"字，为仁之本即做人的根本。

3. The Master said, 'It is rare, indeed, for a man with ***cunning***[1] words and an ***ingratiating***[2] face to be benevolent.'

4. ***Tseng Tzu***[3] said, 'Every day I examine myself on three counts. In what I have ***undertaken***[4] on another's behalf, have I failed to do my best? In my dealings with my friends have I failed to be trustworthy in what I say? Have I passed on to others anything that I have not tried out myself?'

5. The Master said, 'In guiding a state of a thousand ***chariots***[5], approach your duties with reverence and be trustworthy in what you say; avoid excesses in ***expenditure***[6] and love your fellow men; employ the labour of the common people only in the right seasons.'

Notes

1 cunning [ˈkʌniŋ] *a.* 狡诈的，狡猾的

2 ingratiating [inˈgreiʃieitiŋ] *a.* 讨好的，逢迎的

3 Tseng Tzu 曾子，孔子的学生

4 undertake [ˌʌndəˈteik] *v.* 从事，承担

5 chariot [ˈtʃæriət] *n.* 双轮战车

6 expenditure [iksˈpenditʃə] *n.* 开支

3. 子曰：“巧言令色[①]，鲜[②]矣仁。”

孔子说：“总是花言巧语，假装和颜悦色的人，很少是仁慈的。”

4. 曾子[③]曰：“吾日三省吾身[④]。为人谋而不忠乎？与朋友交而不信乎？传不习[⑤]乎？”

曾子说：“我每天都会反省自己很多次，帮别人做事是否尽心尽力？与朋友交往有没有不守信用？学到的知识是否不断温习或应用起来？”

5. 子曰：“道[⑥]千乘之国[⑦]，敬事而信，节用而爱人[⑧]，使民以时。”

孔子说：“治理大国的人应该做到：做事兢兢业业、信守承诺，认真严谨地处理国家政事，节约财政开支，友爱同僚，役使民众而不误他们的农时。”

---

① 巧言令色：朱熹注曰：“好其言，善其色，致饰于外，务以说人。”巧和令都是美好的意思。但此处指装出和颜悦色的样子。

② 鲜：少的意思。

③ 曾子：曾参［shēn］，孔子的重要弟子。

④ 三省吾身：“省”音 xǐng，反省。也可理解为反省三件事，不过根据《论语》的句法，如是此意，“三”字应放在句末：吾日省吾身者三。

⑤ 习：有温习、实习二义。

⑥ 道：治理。

⑦ 千乘之国：有兵车千辆的国家，在当时是大国。乘，音 shèng。

⑧ 爱人：此处的“人”可能指官员或上层人士。下句“使民以时”的“民”字则指民众。

6. The Master said, 'A young man should be a good son at home and an obedient young man abroad, sparing of speech but trustworthy in what he says, and should love the ***multitude***[1] at large but cultivate the friendship of his fellow men. If he has any energy to spare from such action, let him devote it to making himself cultivated.'

7. ***Tzu-hsia***[2] said, 'I would grant that a man has received instruction who appreciates men of excellence where other men appreciate beautiful women, who ***exerts himself***[3] to the ***utmost***[4] in the service of his parents and offers his person to the service of his lord, and who, in his dealings with his friends, is trustworthy in what he says, even though he may say that he has never been taught.'

6. 子曰："弟子[①]入则孝，出则弟[②]，谨而信，泛爱众，而亲仁[③]。行有余力，则以学文。"

孔子说："年轻人在家要孝敬父母，出门要敬爱兄长，为人处事谨慎而又言而有信，尊敬爱护每一个人，亲近有仁德的人。做到了这些并且有余力，就可以继续学习各种文化知识。"

7. 子夏[④]曰："贤贤[⑤]易[⑥]色；事父母，能竭其力；事君，能致其身[⑦]；与朋友交，言而有信。虽曰未学，吾必谓之学矣。"

子夏说："尊敬贤德的人并不断向他们学习，改正自己错误的做法；侍奉父母要尽心尽力；服务君王能全身心地奉献；与朋友交往重诺守义，言而有信。即使这样的人没有读过一天书，我一定说他是很有学问的。"

Notes

1 multitude ['mʌltitju:d] *n.* 群众，大众

2 Tzu-hsia 子夏，孔子的学生。

3 exert oneself 尽力，努力

4 utmost ['ʌtməust] *n.* 最大，极限

① 弟子：可指年轻人或学生，此处指年轻人。

② 出则弟："弟"同"悌"，意为尊敬兄长。

③ 亲仁："仁"指有仁德之人。

④ 子夏：姓卜，名商，字子夏，孔子的学生，比孔子小44岁，生于公元前507年。孔子死后，他在魏国宣传孔子的思想主张。

⑤ 贤贤：第一个"贤"字作动词用，尊重的意思。贤贤即尊重贤者。

⑥ 易：有两种解释；一是改变的意思，此句即为尊重贤者而改正自己错误的做法；二是轻视的意思，即看重贤德而轻视女色。

⑦ 致其身：致，意为"献纳"、"尽力"。这是说把生命奉献给君主。

8. The Master said, 'A gentleman who lacks ***gravity***[1] does not ***inspire***[2] ***awe***[3]. A gentleman who studies is unlikely to be inflexible.

'Make it your guiding principle to do your best for others and to be trustworthy in what you say. Do not accept as friend anyone who is not as good as you.

'When you make a mistake, do not be afraid of mending your ways.'

9. Tseng Tzu said, 'Conduct the funeral of your parents with ***meticulous***[4] care and let not ***sacrifices***[5] to your remote ancestors be forgotten, and the virtue of the common people will incline towards fullness.'

10. ***Tzu-ch'in***[6] asked ***Tzu-kung***[7], 'When the Master arrives in

Notes

1 gravity [ˈɡræviti] *n.* 严肃，庄重

2 inspire [inˈspaiə] *v.* 鼓舞，驱使

3 awe [ɔː] *n.* 敬畏

4 meticulous [miˈtikjuləs] *a.* 谨小慎微的，一丝不苟的

5 sacrifice [ˈsækrifais] *n.* 祭品，献祭

6 Tzu-ch'in 子禽，孔子的学生

7 Tzu-kung 子贡，孔子的学生

8. 子曰："君子不重① 则不威；学则不固②。主忠信③。无④ 友不如己者⑤；过⑥ 则勿惮⑦ 改。"

孔子说："一个人不自重自爱就不会有威严；不断学习才不会鄙陋；恪守忠信，与志同道合的人做朋友，有了过错要去改正，不要害怕改变。"

9. 曾子曰："慎终⑧，追远⑨，民德归厚矣。"

曾子说："慎重地对待丧礼，虔诚地举行祭祀，民风就会慢慢转好的。"

10. 子禽⑩ 问于子贡⑪ 曰："夫子⑫ 至于是邦⑬

---

① 重：庄重、自持。

② 学则不固：有两种解释：一是作坚固解，与上句相连，不庄重就没有威严，所学也不坚固；二是作固陋解，喻人见闻少，学了就可以不固陋。

③ 主忠信：以忠信为主。

④ 无：通毋，"不要"的意思。

⑤ 不如己：一般解释为不如自己。另一种解释说，"不如己者，不类乎己，所谓'道不同不相为谋'也。"把"如"解释为"类似"。后一种解释更为符合孔子的原意。

⑥ 过：过错、过失。

⑦ 惮：音 dàn，害怕、畏惧。

⑧ 慎终：慎重地对待丧礼。终指丧礼。

⑨ 追远：指祭祀时要虔诚。

⑩ 子禽：姓陈，名亢，字子禽。郑玄所注《论语》说他是孔子的学生，但《史记 · 仲尼弟子列传》未载此人，故一说子禽非孔子学生。

⑪ 子贡：姓端木名赐，字子贡，卫国人，比孔子小 31 岁，是孔子的学生，生于公元前 520 年。子贡善辩，孔子认为他可以做大国的宰相。据《史记》记载，子贡在卫国做了商人，家有财产千金，成了有名的商业家。

⑫ 夫子：这是古代的一种敬称，凡是做过大夫的人都可以取得这一称谓。孔子曾担任过鲁国的司寇，所以他的学生们称他为"夫子"。后来，因此而沿袭以称呼老师。《论语》书中所说的"夫子"，都是孔子的学生对他的称呼。

⑬ 邦：指当时割据的诸侯国家。

a state, he ***invariably***[1] gets to know about its government. Does he seek this information? or is it given him?'

Tzu-kung said, 'The Master gets it through being ***cordial***[2], good, respectful, ***frugal***[3] and ***deferential***[4]. The way the Master seeks it is, perhaps, different from the way other men seek it.'

11. The Master said, 'Observe what a man has in mind to do when his father is living, and then observe what he does when his father is dead. If for three years, he makes no changes to his father's ways, he can be said to be a good son.'

12. Yu Tzu said, 'Of the things brought about by the rites, harmony is the most valuable. Of the ways of the Former Kings,

Notes

1 invariably [in'vɛəriəbli] *ad.* 不变地，总是

2 cordial ['kɔ:djəl] *a.* 友好的，真挚的

3 frugal ['fru:gəl] *a.* 节俭的，朴素的

4 deferential [ˌdefə'renʃəl] *a.* 恭敬的

也，必闻其政，求之与，抑① 与之与？”子贡曰：“夫子温、良、恭、俭、让② 以得之。夫子之求之也，其诸③ 异乎人之求之与？”

子禽向子贡请教问题：“老师（孔子）每到一个国家，总是能知道这个国家的政令、政风，这是老师去请求得来的呢？还是有人主动告诉他的呢？”子贡回答说：“老师温良如玉、恭敬俭朴谦让，所以才会有资格知道这些事。老师得到的方法大概与别人的方法不同吧！”

11. 子曰：“父在，观其④ 志；父没，观其行⑤；三年⑥ 无改于父之道⑦，可谓孝矣。”

孔子说：“父亲在世的时候，应该观察儿子的思想、志向；父亲去世以后应该观察儿子的所作所为。如果过了很长的一段时间儿子都没有改变当时的好的作为，就可以说他是很孝顺的了。”

12. 有子曰：“礼之用，和为贵。先王⑧ 之道，斯为美，小大由之。有所不行，知和而和，不

① 抑：表示选择的文言连词，有“还是”的意思。

② 温、良、恭、俭、让：就字面理解即为：温顺、善良、恭敬、俭朴、谦让。这是孔子的弟子对他的赞誉。

③ 其诸：语气词，有“大概”“或者”的意思。

④ 其：他的，指儿子，不是指父亲。

⑤ 行：指行为举止等。

⑥ 三年：指要经过一个较长的时间而已，不一定仅指 3 年的时间。

⑦ 道：有时候是一般意义上的名词，无论好坏、善恶都可以叫作道。但更多时候是积极意义的名词，表示善的、好的东西。这里表示“合理内容”的意思。

⑧ 先王：指尧、舜、禹、汤、文王、武王等圣贤君主。

this is the most beautiful, and is followed alike in matters great and small, yet this will not always work: to aim always at harmony without ***regulating***[1] it by the rites simply because one knows only about harmony will not, in fact, work.'

13. Yu Tzu said, 'To be trustworthy in word is close to being moral in that it enables one's words to be repeated. To be respectful is close to being ***observant***[2] of the rites in that it enables one to stay clear of ***disgrace***[3] and ***insult***[4]. If, in promoting good relationship with relatives by marriage, a man manages not to lose the good will of his own ***kinsmen***[5], he is worthy of being ***looked up to***[6] as the head of the ***clan***[7].'

14. The Master said, 'The gentleman seeks neither a full belly nor a comfortable home. He is quick in action but ***cautious***[8] in speech. He goes to men possessed of the Way to be put right. Such a man can be described as eager to learn.'

以礼节之，亦不可行也。”

有子说：“礼的应用，以和谐为关键。先代圣王的治国方法之最可贵的地方，就在于他们做所有的事都以此为出发点。如果不能做到这一点，只为求和谐的目的而去做，但不以‘礼‘的精髓制约行为，也是行不通的。”

13. 有子曰：“信近① 于义②，言可复③ 也；恭近于礼，远④ 耻辱也；因⑤ 不失其亲，亦可宗⑥ 也。”

有子说：“信守承诺的行为合乎于‘义’，这样的言辞才能够被履行；态度容貌的庄重矜持要符合于礼，这样的行为才不至于遭受侮辱；所依靠的人都是关系亲密、值得依靠的人，这样才可靠。”

14. 子曰：“君子食无求饱，居无求安，敏于事而慎于言，就⑦ 有道⑧ 而正⑨ 焉，可谓好学也已。”

孔子说：“君子（代指一般有德行的人）在

① 近：接近、符合的意思。
② 义：义是儒家的伦理范畴，是指思想和行为符合一定的标准。这个标准就是“礼”。
③ 复：实践的意思。朱熹《集注》云：“复，践言也。”
④ 远：动词，使动用法，使之远离的意思，此外亦可以译为避免。
⑤ 因：依靠、凭藉。一说因应写作姻，但从上下文看似有不妥之处。
⑥ 宗：主、可靠。
⑦ 就：靠近、看齐。
⑧ 有道：指有道德的人。
⑨ 正：匡正、端正。

Notes

1 regulate ['regjuleit] *v.* 调整，制约
2 observant [əb'zə:vənt] *a.* 严格遵守的，符合的
3 disgrace [dis'greis] *n.* 丢脸，不光彩
4 insult [in'sʌlt] *n.* 耻辱，侮辱
5 kinsman ['kinzmən] *n.* 亲属
6 look up to 尊敬
7 clan [klæn] *n.* 宗族，家族
8 cautious ['kɔ:ʃəs] *a.* 小心谨慎的

15. Tzu-kung said, '"Poor without being ***obsequious***[1], wealthy without being ***arrogant***[2]." What do you think of this saying?'

The Master said, 'That will do, but better still "Poor yet delighting in the Way, wealthy yet observant of the ritesrites." '

Tzu-kung said, 'The ***Odes***[3] say,

> Like bone cut, like horn ***polished***[4],
> Like jade ***carved***[5], like stone ground.

Is not what you have said a case in point?'

Notes

1 obsequious [ɔb'siːkwiəs] *a.* 谄媚的

2 arrogant ['ærəgənt] *a.* 骄傲的

3 *Odes* [əud]《诗经》

4 polish ['pɔliʃ] *v.* 磨光

5 carve [kɑːv] *v.* 雕刻

饮食上不求饱足，果腹即可；住所上不求安逸，栖身则已；对事情有敏锐的看法而又慎于言辞，向有道德的人看齐并不断端正自己的行为，这样就算是好学的人了。”

15. 子贡曰：“贫而无谄①，富而无骄，何如②？”子曰：“可也。未若贫而乐③，富而好礼者也。”子贡曰：“《诗》云，‘如切如磋！如琢如磨④’，其斯之谓与？”子曰：“赐⑤也！始可与言《诗》已矣，告诸往而知来者⑥。”

子贡说：“没钱而不谄媚别人；有钱而不骄奢待人，怎么样呀？”孔子说：“这样的人也算是不错了，但是不如虽然贫穷却乐观地生活，富贵而谦恭好礼的人呀！”子贡说：“《诗经》讲，要像对待骨、角、象牙、玉石一样，切磋它，琢磨它，这就是做人或做学问的方法吧？”孔子赞叹道：“赐啊！已经可以和你讲解《诗经》了，你已能从我讲的过去的事情中领会到另外没有说到的意思了。

---

① 谄：音 chǎn，意为巴结、奉承。

② 何如：《论语》书中的“何如”，都可以译为“怎么样”。

③ 贫而乐：一本作“贫而乐道”。

④ 如切如磋，如琢如磨：此二句见《诗经·卫风·淇澳》。有两种解释：一说切磋琢磨分别指对骨、象牙、玉、石 4 种不同材料的加工，否则不能成器；一说加工象牙和骨，切了还要磋，加工玉石，琢了还要磨，有精益求精之意。

⑤ 赐：子贡名，孔子对学生都称其名。

⑥ 告诸往而知来者：诸，同之；往，过去的事情；来，未来的事情。

16. The Master said, 'It is not the failure of others to appreciate your abilities that should trouble you, but rather your failure to appreciate theirs.'

16. 子曰：“不患[1]人[2]之不已知，患不知人也。”

孔子说：“不担心别人不知道自己，而担心自己不了解别人啊！”

① 患：忧虑、担心。
② 人：指有教养、有知识的人。

Book II

1. The Master said, 'The rule of virtue can be compared to the Pole Star which ***commands***[1] the ***homage***[2] of the multitude of stars without leaving its place.'

2. The Master said, 'The *Odes* are three hundred in number. They can be ***summed***[3] up in one phrase,

Swerving[4] not from the right path.'[*]

* This line is from Ode 297 where it describes a team of horses going straight ahead without swerving to left or right.

卷 二

Notes

1 command [kə'mɑ:nd] *v.* 命令

2 homage ['hɔmidʒ] *n.* 尊敬

3 sum [sʌm] *v.* 总和，概括

4 swerve [swə:v] *v.* 背离

1. 子曰："为政以德[①]，譬如北辰[②]，居其所而众星共[③]之。"

孔子说："如果君王以'德'治理国家，那就会像北极星一样，安居在自己的位置而其余众星有序地环绕在它的周围（随它的方向前进）。"

2. 子曰："《诗》三百[④]，一言以蔽之，曰：'思无邪[⑤]。'"

孔子说："《诗经》的全部内容用一句话来概括就是：思想纯正。"

---

① 为政以德：以，用的意思。此句是说统治者应以道德进行统治，即"德治"。

② 北辰：北极星。

③ 共：同拱，环绕。

④ 《诗》三百：《诗经》中有305篇诗，说"《诗》三百"是说一整数。

⑤ "思无邪"：这是《诗经·鲁颂》中的一句，孔子借来概括《诗经》的内容。

3. The Master said, 'Guide them by ***edicts***[1], keep them in line with punishments, and the common people will stay out of trouble but will have no sense of shame. Guide them by virtue, keep them in line with the rites, and they will, besides having a sense of shame, ***reform***[2] themselves.'

4. The Master said, 'At fifteen I set my heart on learning; at thirty I took my stand; at forty I came to be free from doubts; at fifty I understood the ***Decree of Heaven***[3]; at sixty my ear was ***attuned***[4];* at seventy I followed my heart's desire without ***overstepping***[5] the line.'

5. Meng Yi Tzu asked about being ***filial***[6]. The Master answered, 'Never fail to comply.'

---

* The expression *erh shun* is very obscure and the translation is tentative.

Notes

1 edict ['i:dikt] *n.* 命令，法令

2 reform [ri'fɔ:m] *v.* 改革，改正

3 Decree of Heaven 天命

4 attuned [ə'tju:nd] *a.* 乐感好的；理解的

5 overstep ['əuvəstep] *v.* 违反，逾越

6 filial ['filiəl] *a.* 子女的，孝顺的

3. 子曰："道① 之以政，齐之以刑，民免而无耻；道之以德，齐之以礼，有耻且格②。"

孔子说："如果用行政命令来训导民众，用严刑峻法来整束民众，民众只会千方百计避免获罪而丧失廉耻之心；如果用道德引导民众，用礼仪约束民众，民众就会有羞耻之心并且努力（改正自己）以达到要求。"

4. 子曰："吾十有③ 五而志于学，三十而立④，四十而不惑⑤，五十而知天命⑥，六十而耳顺⑦，七十而从心所欲不逾矩⑧。"

孔子说："我 15 岁的时候立下了学习的志向，30 岁时说话做事有了把握，40 岁时掌握了知识，开始不为外界事物困惑，50 岁时知晓天命，60 岁对不利于自己的意见也会正确对待，70 岁以后则能行动都随自己的心意而又不会越过世俗规矩。"

5. 孟懿子⑨ 问孝。子曰："无违⑩。"樊迟⑪ 御，

---

① 道：同"导"。

② 格：符合规格，达到要求。

③ 有：同"又"。

④ 立：站得住的意思。

⑤ 不惑：掌握了知识，不被外界事物而困惑。

⑥ 天命：指不能为人力所支配的事情。

⑦ 耳顺：对此有多种解释。一般而言，指对那些于己不利的意见也能正确对待。

⑧ 从心所欲不逾矩：从，遵从的意思；逾，越过；矩，规矩。

⑨ 孟懿子：鲁国的大夫，复姓仲孙或孟孙，故下文称孟孙。

⑩ 无违：古人常用"违"来指违礼。

⑪ 樊迟：名须，字子迟，孔子的学生。

Fan Ch'ih[1] was driving. The Master told him about the interview, saying, 'Meng-sun asked me about being filial. I answered, "Never fail to comply."'

Fan Ch'ih asked, 'What does that mean?'

The Master said, 'When your parents are alive, comply with the rites in serving them; when they die, ***comply***[2] with the rites in burying them; comply with the rites in sacrificing to them.'

6. ***Meng Wu Po***[3] asked about being filial. The Master said, 'Give your father and mother no other cause for ***anxiety***[4] than illness.'

7. Tzu-yu asked about being filial. The Master said, 'Nowadays for a man to be filial means no more than that he is able to provide his parents with food. Even hounds and horses are, in some way, provided with food. If a man shows no ***reverence***[5], where is the difference?'

Notes

1 Fan Ch'ih 樊迟，孔子的学生

2 comply [kəm'plai] v. 遵守

3 Meng Wu Po 孟武伯，孟懿子的儿子

4 anxiety [æn'zaiəti] n. 担忧

5 reverence ['revərəns] n. 尊敬

子告之曰："孟孙问孝于我，我对曰'无违'。"樊迟曰："何谓也？"子曰："生，事之以礼；死，葬之以礼，祭之以礼。"

孟懿子向孔子请教关于"孝"的问题。孔子回答他说："不要违背。"当樊迟为孔子驾车的时候，孔子告诉他说："孟孙（孟懿子）问我什么是孝，我告诉他说就是'不要违背'。"樊迟问道："这是什么意思呢？"孔子回答道："当父母在世的时候，以礼来侍奉他们，父母过世了，以礼来安葬他们，以礼来祭祀怀念他们。"

6. 孟武伯① 问孝，子曰："父母唯其疾之忧②。"

孟武伯问孔子什么是"孝"，孔子回答说："孝顺父母就是要（时刻）关心他们的身体，为他们的疾病担忧。"

7. 子游③ 问孝，子曰："今之孝者，是谓能养。至于犬马，皆能有养④，不敬，何以别乎？"

子游向孔子请教什么是"孝"，孔子说："今天我们说到'孝'，就说是能够赡养老人就可以了。但我们对家里的狗、马也能做到很好地喂养它们；所以，如果没有用恭敬的态度对待父母，那么这种赡养与喂养家里的动物有什么区别呢？"

---

① 孟武伯：孟懿子的儿子，名彘，音 zhì。武是他的谥号。

② 父母唯其疾之忧：其，代词，指父母。疾，病。

③ 子游：姓言名偃，字子游，孔子的学生。

④ 养：指饲养。

8. Tzu-hsia asked about being filial. The Master said, 'What is difficult to manage is the ***expression***[1] on one's face. As for the young taking on the burden when there is work to be done or letting the old enjoy the wine and the food when these are ***available***[2], that hardly ***deserves***[3] to be called filial.'

9. The Master said, 'I can speak to Hui all day without his disagreeing with me in any way. Thus he would seem to be stupid. However, when I take a closer look at what he does in private after he has ***withdrawn***[4] from my presence, I discover that it does, in fact, ***throw light on***[5] what I said. Hui is not stupid after all.'

10. The Master said, 'Look at the means a man employs, observe the path he takes and ***examine***[6] where he feels at home. In

Notes

1 expression [iks'preʃən] *n.* 表情

2 available [ə'veiləbl] *a.* 可实现的，可得到的

3 deserve [di'zə:v] *v.* 应得，值得

4 withdraw [wið'drɔ:] *v.* 离开，退出

5 throw light on 阐明…

6 examine [ig'zæmin] *v.* 检查，考查

8. 子夏问孝，子曰："色难①。有事，弟子服其劳②；有酒食，先生③馔④，曾是以为孝乎？"

子夏问孔子什么是"孝"。孔子说："要做到和颜悦色、始终恭敬最不容易。如果只是父母长辈有什么事，晚辈子女帮他们完成、服侍他们；有好的饮食也都先拿来奉给他们，你以为这样就是做到'孝'了吗？"

9. 子曰："吾与回⑤言，终日不违⑥，如愚。退而省其私⑦，亦足以发，回也不愚。"

孔子说："每次我跟颜回说些什么，一整天他都不会提出什么相反的意见或问题来，就好像很愚钝一样。但通过观察他私下里与其他人的言行，其实对我们平时讨论的问题有很多阐发。颜回也并不是很愚钝呀！"

10. 子曰："视其所以⑧，观其所由⑨，察其所安⑩，人焉廋⑪哉？人焉廋哉？"

孔子说："（要考察一个人）只要看他所做

① 色难：色，脸色。难，不容易的意思。
② 服劳：服，从事、担负。服劳即服侍。
③ 先生：先生指长者或父母；前面说的弟子，指晚辈、儿女等。
④ 馔：音 zhuàn，意为饮食、吃喝。
⑤ 回：姓颜名回，字子渊，生于公元前 521 年，比孔子小 30 岁，鲁国人，孔子的得意门生。
⑥ 不违：不提相反的意见和问题。
⑦ 退而省其私：考察颜回私下里与其他学生讨论学问的言行。
⑧ 所以：所做的事情。
⑨ 所由：所经历的事情。
⑩ 所安：所安的心境。
⑪ 廋：音 sōu，隐藏、藏匿。

what way is a man's true character hidden from view? In what way is a man's true character hidden from view?'

11. The Master said, 'A man is worthy of being a teacher who gets to know what is new by keeping ***fresh***[1] in his mind what he is already familiar with.'

12. The Master said, 'The gentleman is no ***vessel***[2].'*

13. Tzu-kung asked about the gentleman. The Master said, 'He puts his words into action before allowing his words to follow his action.'

14. The Master said, 'The gentleman enters into ***associations***[3] but not ***cliques***[4]; the small man enters into cliques but not associations.'

15. The Master said, 'If one learns from others but does not think, one will be ***bewildered***[5]. If, on the other hand, one thinks but does not learn from others, one will be in ***peril***[6].'

* i.e., he is no specialist, as every vessel is designed for a specific purpose only.

Notes

1 fresh [freʃ] *a.* 新的

2 vessel [ˈvesəl] *n.* 容器，器皿

3 association [əˌsəuʃiˈeiʃən] *n.* 联盟，合群

4 clique [klik] *n.* 派系，勾结

5 bewilder [biˈwildə] *v.* 使迷惑

6 peril [ˈperil] *n.* 危险

过的事情，观察他曾经的经历，看他的秉性涵养，这样一个人怎么能掩藏自己呢？怎么能掩藏自己呢？"

11. 子曰："温故而知新①，可以为师矣。"

孔子说："不断温习以前学到的知识，不断从中阐发出新的体会，这样的人可以做老师了。"

12. 子曰："君子不器②。"

孔子说："君子不会像器皿一样，只具备某一方面的才能。"

13. 子贡问君子。子曰："先行其言而后从之。"

子贡问孔子怎样做一个君子。孔子说："对于要说的话，先将它付诸于行动，然后再将它说出来（这样才是君子）。"

14. 子曰："君子周③而不比④，小人⑤比而不周。"

孔子说："君子与人相处合群而不勾结，小人则是与人勾结而不合群。"

15. 子曰："学而不思则罔⑥，思而不学

---

① 温故而知新：故，过去的。新，刚刚学到的知识或新的体会。

② 器：器具。孔子用"君子不器"来主张君子要具备多种才能和技艺。

③ 周：合群。

④ 比：音 bì，勾结。

⑤ 小人：没有道德修养的凡人。

⑥ 罔：迷惑、糊涂。

16. The Master said, 'To ***attack***[1] a task from the wrong end can do nothing but harm.'

17. The Master said, '***Yu***[2], shall I tell you what it is to know. To say you know when you know, and to say you do not when you do not, that is knowledge.'

18. Tzu-chang was studying with an eye to an official career. The Master said, 'Use your ears widely but leave out what is ***doubtful***[3]; repeat the rest with caution and you will make few mistakes. Use your eyes widely and leave out what is ***hazardous***[4]; put the rest into practice with caution and you will have few ***regrets***[5]. When in your speech you make few mistakes and in your action you have few regrets, an official career will follow as a matter of course.'

Notes

1 attack [ə'tæk] *v.* 攻击

2 Yu 由，子路，孔子的学生

3 doubtful ['dautful] *a.* 怀疑的，使人产生疑问的

4 hazardous ['hæzədəs] *a.* 有危险的

5 regret [ri'gret] *n.* 遗憾，后悔

则殆①。”

孔子说：“单纯学习知识但不去思索，就会感到茫然、迷惑，只是不断空想但不学习实践，就会感到迷惑、茫然。”

16. 子曰：“攻② 乎异端③，斯④ 害也已⑤。”

孔子说：“（不讲道理地）攻击反对不同于己的言论或事物，这种行为也是错误的。”

17. 子曰：“由⑥，诲女⑦，知之乎？知之为知之，不知为不知，是知也。”

孔子说：由啊，我教导你的你明白吗？对一件事，知道就是知道，不知道就是不知道，这就是有智慧啊。

18. 子张⑧学干禄⑨，子曰：“多闻阙⑩疑⑪，慎言其余，则寡尤⑫；多见阙殆，慎行其余，则寡悔。言寡尤，行寡悔，禄在其中矣。”

子张问怎样求取官职。孔子回答说：“多听

① 殆：疑惑、危险。
② 攻：攻击。有人将“攻”解释为“治”。不妥。
③ 异端：不正确的言论。另外、不同的一端。
④ 斯：代词，这。
⑤ 也已：这里用作语气词。
⑥ 由：姓仲名由，字子路。生于公元前542年，孔子的学生。
⑦ 女：同汝，你。
⑧ 子张：姓颛孙名师，字子张，生于公元前503年，比孔子小48岁，孔子的学生。
⑨ 干禄：干，求的意思。禄，即古代官吏的俸禄。干禄就是求取官职。
⑩ 阙：缺。此处意为放置在一旁。
⑪ 疑：怀疑。
⑫ 寡尤：寡，少的意思。尤，过错。

19. ***Duke Ai***[1] asked, 'What must I do before the common people will look up to me?'

Confucius[2] answered, 'Raise the straight and set them over the ***crooked***[3] and the common people will look up to you. Raise the crooked and set them over the straight and the common people will not look up to you.'

20. ***Chi K'ang Tzu***[4] asked, 'How can one ***inculcate***[5] in the common people the virtue of reverence, of doing their best and of ***enthusiasm***[6]?'

The Master said, 'Rule over them with ***dignity***[7] and they will be reverent; treat them with kindness and they will do their best; raise the good and instruct those who are backward and they will be ***imbued***[8] with enthusiasm.'

取别人的意见，有疑问的就先将它搁置在一边，对有把握的事也不要轻易地谈论，这样说话就会少犯错误；遇到事情要多观察，有怀疑的就先不做，对有把握的事也要谨慎地去处理，这样做事就不会有太多悔恨。做到了少说错话、少做错事，官职俸禄自然就能得到。”

19. 哀公① 问曰：“何为则民服？”孔子对曰②：“举直错诸枉③，则民服；举枉错诸直，则民不服。”

鲁哀公问孔子：“怎样做才能使民众臣服？”孔子回答说：“选拔任用正直公平的人，把不正直的人放置一旁，那么人民就会臣服；任用不正直的人而将正直无私的人放置不予任用，则民众不会臣服。”

20. 季康子④ 问：“使民敬、忠以⑤ 劝⑥，如之何？”子曰：“临⑦ 之以庄，则敬；孝慈⑧，则忠；举善而教不能，则劝。”

---

① 哀公：姓姬名蒋，哀是其谥号，鲁国国君，公元前 494～公元前 468 年在位。

② 对曰：《论语》中记载，对国君及在上位者问话的回答，都用“对曰”，以表示尊敬。

③ 举直错诸枉：举，选拔的意思。直，正直公平。错，同措，放置。枉，不正直。

④ 季康子：姓季孙名肥，康是他的谥号，鲁哀公时任正卿，是当时政治上最有权势的人。

⑤ 以：连接词，与“而”同。

⑥ 劝：勉励。这里是自勉努力的意思。

⑦ 临：对待。

⑧ 孝慈：一说当政者自己孝慈；一说当政者引导老百姓孝慈。此处采用后者。

Notes

1 Duke Ai 哀公，鲁国国君

2 Confucius [kən'fju:ʃəs] 孔子

3 crooked ['krukid] *a.* 不直的，弯曲的；不正直的

4 Chi K‘ang Tzu 季康子，鲁哀公时任正卿，当时政治上最有权势的人

5 inculcate [in'kʌlkeit] *v.* 灌输，教导

6 enthusiasm [in'θju:ziæzəm] *n.* 热心；〈古〉虔诚

7 dignity ['digniti] *n.* 威严，端庄

8 imbue [im'bju:] *v.* 使充满；鼓舞

21. Someone said to Confucius, 'Why do you not take part in government?"

The Master said, '***The Book of History***[1] says, "Oh! Simply by being a good son and friendly to his brothers a man can ***exert***[2] an influence upon government." In so doing a man is, in fact, taking part in government. How can there be any question of his having actively to "take part in government"?'

22. The Master said, 'I do not see how a man can be acceptable who is untrustworthy in word. When a ***pin***[3] is missing in the ***yoke-bar***[4] of a large cart or in the ***collar-bar***[5] of a small ***cart***[6], how can the cart be expected to go?'

Notes

1 *The Book of History* 《尚书》

2 exert [ig'zə:t] *v.* 施加，产生（影响）

3 pin [pin] *n.* 针，古代大车横木上的木销子

4 yoke-bar *n.*（大车上的）车辕前面的横木

5 collar-bar *n.*（小车上的）车辕前面的横木

6 cart [kɑ:t] *n.* 二轮运货马车

季康子问孔子："要使民众恭敬、忠厚，并且自勉努力，应该怎样做呢？"孔子说："对待民众庄重威严，他们就会态度恭敬；通过自己的行为引导百姓孝敬父母、慈爱兄弟，则民风忠厚；提拔良善的人而教导能力差的人，人们就会自勉努力了。"

21. 或[①]谓孔子曰："子奚[②]不为政？"子曰："《书》[③]云：'孝乎惟孝，友于兄弟，施于有政[④]。'是亦为政，奚其为为政？"

有人对孔子说："先生为什么不从事政治呢？"孔子回答道："《尚书》里说过，孝就是孝敬父母，友爱兄弟。把这孝的风气去影响当政者，也就是从政了，难道只有做官才能算是从事政治吗？"

22. 子曰："人而无信，不知其可也。大车无輗[⑤]，小车无軏[⑥]，其何以行之哉？"

孔子说："一个人做事没有信誉，会让人不知道他到底想做什么，让人无所适从。就像牛车上没有輗，小车上没有軏一样，它凭什么来行进呢？"

---

① 或：有人。不定代词。

② 奚：疑问词，相当于"为什么"。

③ 《书》：指《尚书》。

④ 施于有政：施：一作施行讲；一作延及讲。

⑤ 輗：音 ní，古代大车车辕前面横木上的木销子。大车指的是牛车。

⑥ 軏：音 yuè，古代小车车辕前面横木上的木销子。没有輗和軏，车就不能走。

23. Tzu-chang asked, 'Can ten generations ***hence***[1] be known?'

The Master said, 'The Yin built on the rites of the Hsia. What was added and what was ***omitted***[2] can be known. The Chou built on the rites of the Yin. What was added and what was omitted can be known. Should there be a ***successor***[3] to the Chou, even a hundred generations hence can be known.'

24. The Master said, 'To offer sacrifice to the spirit of an ancestor not one's own is obsequious.

'Faced with what is right, to leave it ***undone***[4] shows a lack of courage.'

Notes

1 hence [hens] *ad.* 因此

2 omit [əu'mit] *v.* 省略

3 successor [sək'sesə] *n.* 继承者

4 undone [ʌn'dʌn] *a.* 没做的

23. 子张问："十世① 可知也？" 子曰："殷因② 于夏礼，所损益③ 可知也；周因于殷礼，所损益可知也。其或继周者，虽百世，可知也。"

子张问孔子："今后十世（的礼仪制度）可以知道吗？" 孔子回答说："殷代沿用夏代的礼制，周代沿用殷代的礼制，他们在因循的过程中对这些礼制的修整变化是可以考察到的。以后别的继承周代的国家就算历任百世，他的礼制也可以推出来。"

24. 子曰："非其鬼④ 而祭之；谄⑤ 也。见义⑥ 不为，无勇也。"

孔子说："不是自己家的祖先而去祭祀他，这是谄媚的行为，见到应该做的事而不做，是没有勇气。"

---

① 世：古时称 30 年为一世。也有的把"世"解释为朝代。

② 因：因袭：沿用、继承。

③ 损益：减少和增加，即优化、变动之义。

④ 鬼：有两种解释：一是指鬼神，二是指死去的祖先。

⑤ 谄：音 chǎn，谄媚、阿谀。

⑥ 义：人应该做的事就是义。

Book III

1. Confucius said of the Chi Family, 'They use eight rows of eight dancers each* to perform in their courtyard. If this can be ***tolerated***[1], what cannot be tolerated?'

2. ***The Three Families***[2†] performed the ***yung***[3‡] when the sacrificial offerings were being cleared away. The Master said,

'In ***attendance***[4] were the great lords,
In ***solemn***[5] dignity was the ***Emperor***[6].
What application has this to the halls of the Three Families?'

---

* A prerogative of the Emperor.

† The three noble families of the state of Lu: Meng-sun, Shu-sun and Chi-sun.

‡ Ode 282, from which the couplet quoted comes.

卷　三

Notes

1 tolerate ['tɔləreit] *v.* 忍受

2 The Three Families 鲁家当政的三家

3 *yung* 《雍》

4 attendance [ə'tendəns] *n.* 在场，出席

5 solemn ['sɔləm] *a.* 庄严的

6 emperor ['empərə] *n.* 皇帝，天子

1. 孔子谓季氏①："八佾②舞于庭，是可忍③，孰不可忍也！"

孔子评论季平子说："季家用违反礼仪的八佾在自家庭院里演出，这种事情都容忍做出来了，还有什么事做不出来呢？"

2. 三家④者以《雍》⑤彻。子曰："'相维辟公，天子穆穆'⑥，奚取于三家之堂⑦"。

---

① 季氏：鲁国正卿季孙氏，即季平子。

② 八佾：佾音 yì，行列的意思。古时一佾八人，八佾就是 64 人，据《周礼》规定，只有周天子才可以使用八佾，诸侯为六佾，卿大夫为四佾，士用二佾。季氏是正卿，只能用四佾。

③ 可忍：可以容忍。一说可以忍心。

④ 三家：鲁国当政的三家：孟孙氏、叔孙氏、季孙氏。他们都是鲁桓公的后代，又称"三桓"。

⑤ 《雍》：《诗经·周颂》中的一篇。古代天子祭宗庙完毕撤去祭品时唱这首诗。

⑥ 相维辟公，天子穆穆：《雍》诗中的两句。相，助。维，语助词，无意义。辟公，指诸侯。穆穆：庄严肃穆。

⑦ 堂：接客祭祖的地方。

3. The Master said, 'What can a man do with the rites who is not ***benevolent***[1]? What can a man do with music who is not benevolent?'

4. Lin Fang asked about the basis of the rites. The Master said, 'A noble question indeed! With the rites, it is better to ***err on the side of***[2] ***frugality***[3] than on the side of ***extravagance***[4]; in ***mourning***[5], it is better to err on the side of grief than on the side of ***formality***[6].'

5. The Master said, '***Barbarian***[7] tribes with their rulers are inferior to Chinese states without them.'

在鲁国当政的孟孙氏、叔孙氏、季孙氏三家在祭祖完毕撤去祭品时，也命乐工唱《雍》这篇诗。孔子评论说："'(诗《雍》中的两句)'助祭的是诸侯，天子严肃静穆地在那里主祭。这样的意思，怎么能用在你们3家祭祖的庙堂里呢？"

3. 子曰："人而不仁，如礼何？人而不仁，如乐何？"

孔子说："为人没有仁德，他要怎样实行礼制呢？为人没有仁德，他要怎样运用乐制呢？"

4. 林放[①] 问礼之本。子曰："大哉问！礼，与其奢也，宁俭；丧，与其易[②] 也，宁戚[③]。"

林放向孔子询问"礼"的根本。孔子回答说："这是多么重要的问题呀！礼仪，与其奢侈宁愿俭朴；丧礼，与其仪式铺张不如内心悲戚。"

5. 子曰："夷狄[④] 之有君，不如诸夏[⑤] 之亡[⑥] 也。"

孔子说："蛮荒之地的人即使有君主统治，也不如中原礼仪之邦的人没有君主统治。"

---

① 林放：鲁国人。

② 易：治理。这里指有关丧葬的礼节仪式办理得很周到。一说谦和、平易。

③ 戚：心中悲哀的意思。

④ 夷狄：古代中原地区的人对周边地区的贬称，谓之不开化，缺乏教养，不知书达礼。

⑤ 诸夏：古代中原地区华夏族的自称。

⑥ 亡：同无。古书中的"无"字多写作"亡"。

Notes

1 benevolent [bi'nevələnt] *a.* 仁慈的，善意的

2 err on the side of 按某种特定偏向行事

3 frugality [fruː'gæliti] *n.* 节俭

4 extravagance [ik'strævəgəns] *n.* 铺张，浪费

5 mourning ['mɔːniŋ] *n.* 悲伤，服丧

6 formality [fɔː'mæliti] *n.* 仪式，礼节

7 barbarian [bɑː'bɛəriən] *a.* 野蛮的，不开化的

6. The Chi Family were going to perform the sacrifice to Mount T'ai.[*] The Master said to ***Jan Ch'iu***[1],[†] 'Can you not save the situation?'

'No. I cannot.'

The Master said, 'Alas! Who would have thought that Mount T'ai would suffer in ***comparison***[2] with Lin Fang?'[‡]

7. The Master said, 'There is no ***contention***[3] between gentlemen. The nearest to it is, perhaps, ***archery***[4]. In archery they bow and make way for one another as they go up and on coming down they drink together. Even the way they contend is gentlemanly.'

8. Tzu-hsia asked,

'Her entrancing smile ***dimpling***[5],
Her beautiful eyes ***glancing***[6],
Patterns of colour upon ***plain***[7] silk.

What is the meaning of these lines?'

The Master said, 'The colours are put in after the white.'

'Does the practice of the rites ***likewise***[8] come afterwards?'

The Master said, 'It is you, Shang, who have thrown light on

---

* Not being the lord of the state of Lu, the head of the Chi Family was not entitled to perform the sacrifice to Mount TTai and it would be a violation of the rites for Mount TTai to accept the sacrifice.

† Who was in the service of the Chi Family.

‡ See III. 4 above where Lin Fang showed a concern for the basis of the rites.

Notes

1 Jan Ch'iu 冉有，字子有，孔子的学生

2 comparison [kəm'pærizən] *n.* 比较

3 contention [kən'tenʃən] *n.* 争论；竞争

4 archery ['ɑːtʃəri] *n.* 射箭

5 dimple ['dimpl] *v.* 出现酒窝

6 glance [glɑːns] *v.* 一瞥；闪烁

7 plain [plein] *a.* 朴素的；素的

8 likewise ['laikwaiz] *ad.* 也

6. 季氏旅① 于泰山，子谓冉有② 曰："女③ 弗能救④ 与？"对曰："不能。"子曰："呜呼！曾谓泰山不如林放⑤ 乎？"

季氏将要祭祀泰山，孔子问冉有："你难道不能劝阻他这种不合礼制的行为吗？"冉有回答说："不能。"孔子叹道："哎！难道泰山神还不如林放知礼，而会接受不合规矩的祭礼吗？"

7. 子曰："君子无所争，必也射⑥ 乎！揖⑦ 让而升，下而饮，其争也君子。"

孔子说："君子没有什么争强好胜的心，如果有的话，那就在射箭比赛上表现最明显了。开始比赛时，先拱手行礼以示尊敬，相互礼让后上场，射完箭又相互作揖，再退下来一起喝酒。这种争的方式也是君子的做法。"

8. 子夏问曰："'巧笑倩兮，美目盼兮，素以为绚兮'。⑧ 何谓也？"子曰："绘事后素⑨。"曰：

---

① 旅：祭名。祭祀山川为旅。当时，只有天子和诸侯才有祭祀名山大川的资格。

② 冉有：姓冉名求，字子有，生于公元前 522 年，孔子的弟子，比孔子小 29 岁。当时是季氏的家臣，所以孔子责备他。

③ 女：同汝，你。

④ 救：挽求、劝阻的意思。这里指谏止。

⑤ 林放：见本卷第 4 段之注。

⑥ 射：原意为射箭。此处指古代的射礼。

⑦ 揖：拱手行礼，表示尊敬。

⑧ 巧笑倩兮，美目盼兮，素以为绚兮：前两句见《诗经·卫风·硕人》篇。倩，音 qiàn，笑得好看。兮，语助词，相当于"啊"。盼：眼睛黑白分明。绚，有文采。

⑨ 绘事后素：绘，画。素，白底。

the text for me. Only with a man like you can one discuss the *Odes*.'

9. The Master said, 'I am able to ***discourse***[1] on the rites of the Hsia, but the state of Ch'i does not ***furnish***[2] ***sufficient***[3] supporting evidence; I am able to discourse on the rites of the Yin, but the state of Sung does not furnish sufficient supporting evidence. This is because there are not enough records and men of ***erudition***[4]. Otherwise I would be able to support what I say with evidence.'

10. The Master said, 'I do not wish to ***witness***[5] that part of the *ti* sacrifice[*] which follows the opening ***libation***[6] to the ***impersonator***[7].'[†]

* An important sacrifice performed by the Emperor, but the privilege of performing it was granted to the Duke of Chou, the founder of the state of Lu.

† The young boy or girl who impersonates the dead ancestor to whom the offerings are made.

Notes

1 discourse ['diskɔ:s] *v.* 讲述

2 furnish ['fə:niʃ] *v.* 提供

3 sufficient [sə'fiʃənt] *a.* 足够的

4 erudition [ˌeru'diʃən] *n.* 博学

5 witness ['witnis] *v.* 见证

6 libation [lai'beiʃən] *n.* 奠酒（祭神仪式）

7 impersonator [im'pə:səneitə] *n.* 演员

"礼后乎？"子曰："起予者商也[①]，始可与言《诗》已矣。"

子夏问孔子说："《诗经》上说，乖巧的笑容多迷人，美丽的眼睛多灵动，用素粉来打扮多漂亮啊。这几句话是什么意思呢？"孔子回答道："这是说先有白底然后才能画画。"子夏又问道："那么说礼也是后起的事了？"孔子答道："商，你真是能启发我的人，现在可以同你一起讨论《诗经》了。"

9. 子曰："夏礼吾能言之，杞[②]不足征[③]也；殷礼吾能言之，宋[④]不足征也。文献[⑤]不足故也。足，则吾能征之矣。"

孔子说："夏代的礼制我还能说出来，但单凭杞国现存的礼制已不足以证明我所说的了；殷代的礼制我能说出来，但凭宋国的礼制也已经不能证明我所说的了。这是因为他们所保留下来的文献资料不足的缘故啊。如果资料足够的话，我就能证明给你们看了。"

10. 子曰："禘[⑥]自既灌[⑦]而往者，吾不欲观

---

① 起予者商也：起，启发。予，我，孔子自指。商，子夏名商。

② 杞：春秋时国名，是夏禹的后裔。在今河南杞县一带。

③ 征：证明。

④ 宋：春秋时国名，是商汤的后裔，在今河南商丘一带。

⑤ 文献：文，指历史典籍；献，指贤人。

⑥ 禘：音 dì，古代只有天子才可以举行的祭祀祖先的非常隆重的典礼。

⑦ 灌：禘礼中第一次献酒。

11. Someone asked about the theory of the *ti* sacrifice. The Master said, 'It is not something I understand, for whoever understands it will be able to manage the Empire as easily as if he had it here.' pointing to his ***palm***[1].

12. '***Sacrifice***[2] as if present' is taken to mean 'sacrifice to the gods as if the gods were present.'

The Master, however, said, 'Unless I take part in a sacrifice, it is as if I did not sacrifice.'

13. ***Wang-sun Chia***[3] said,

'Better to be obsequious to the kitchen stove
Than to the southwest corner of the house.*

What does that mean?'

The Master said, 'The saying has got it wrong. When you have offended against Heaven, there is nowhere you can turn to in your ***prayers***[4].'

---

* By 'the southwest corner of the house', which is the place of honour, Wang-sun Chia, being a minister of Wei, presumably meant to refer to the lord of Wei and by 'the kitchen stove' to himself.

Notes

1 palm [pɑːm] *n.* 手掌

2 sacrifice ['sækrifais] *n.* 祭献，供奉

3 Wang-sun Chia 王孙贾，卫灵公的大臣

4 prayer [prɛə] *n.* 祈祷，祷告

之矣[①]。"

孔子说："对于行禘礼的仪式，从第一次献酒以后，我就不愿意再往下看了。"

11. 或问禘之说[②]，子曰："不知也。知其说者之于天下也，其如示诸斯[③]乎！"指其掌。

有人向孔子询问关于禘祭的规定，孔子回答说："我不知道。真正懂得禘这个文化精神的人，看天下国家事物的道理，就好像是呈现在这里这么清楚明白。"说完指指掌心。

12. 祭如在，祭神如神在。子曰："吾不与祭，如不祭。"

祭祀祖先就要像祖宗在自己面前一样（恭敬），祭神就要像真正面对神灵一样虔诚。孔子说："如果我没有全心投入到祭祀中去，不如不去祭祀。"

13. 王孙贾[④]问曰："与其媚[⑤]于奥[⑥]，宁媚于灶[⑦]，何谓也？"子曰："不然。获罪于天[⑧]，无所祷也。"

卫国大臣王孙贾问孔子："（有人说）与其向奥神献媚，不如向灶神献媚，这是什么意

---

① 吾不欲观之矣：我不愿意看了。
② 禘之说："说"，理论、道理、规定。禘之说，意为关于禘祭的规定。
③ 示诸斯："斯"指后面的"掌"字。
④ 王孙贾：卫灵公的大臣，时任大夫。
⑤ 媚：谄媚、巴结、奉承。
⑥ 奥：这里指屋内位居西南角的神。
⑦ 灶：这里指灶旁管烹饪做饭的神。
⑧ 天：以天喻君，一说天即理。

14. The Master said, 'The Chou is ***resplendent***[1] in culture, having before it the example of the two ***previous***[2] ***dynasties***[3].[*] I am for the ***Chou***[4].'

15. When the Master went inside ***the Grand Temple***[5],[†] he asked questions about everything. Someone ***remarked***[6], 'Who said that the son of the man from ***Tsou***[7‡] understood the ***rites***[8]? When he went inside the Grand Temple, he asked questions about everything.'

The Master, on hearing of this, said, 'The asking of questions is in itself the correct rite.'

16. The Master said,

'In archery the point lies not in ***piercing***[9] the hide.[§]

For the reason that strength varies from man to man.

This was the way of antiquity.'

---

* The Hsia and the Yin.

† The temple of the Duke of Chou, the founder of the state of Lu.

‡ The man from Tsou refers to Confucius' father.

§ i.e., the bull's eye fixed in the centre of a cloth target.

思？”孔子回答道：“不是这样的。当所做的事为天理难容时，无论向谁祈祷都没有用。”

14. 子曰：“周监[①]于二代[②]，郁郁[③]乎文哉，吾从周。”

孔子说：“周代承继借鉴了夏商两朝的礼仪文化，礼制文化非常丰富、伟大与光辉，我遵从周代的礼制。”

15. 子入太庙[④]，每事问。或曰：“孰谓鄹[⑤]人之子知礼乎？入太庙，每事问。”子闻之，曰：“是礼也。”

孔子到了太庙，每遇一件事都会详细询问。有人说：“不是说孔子对礼制很有研究吗？那为什么进了太庙事无巨细都要询问呢？”孔子听到后说：“这件事（对每一件事都详细询问）本身就是懂礼制的表现啊！”

16. 子曰：“射不主皮[⑥]，为力不同科[⑦]，古之道也。”

孔子说：“比赛射箭时不在于能让箭穿透靶子，因为各人的力气大小不同。这是自古以来就有的规矩。”

① 监：音 jiàn，同鉴，借鉴的意思。
② 二代：这里指夏代和商代。
③ 郁郁：文采盛貌。丰富、浓郁之意。
④ 太庙：君主的祖庙。鲁国太庙，即周公旦的庙，供鲁国祭祀周公。
⑤ 鄹：音 zōu，春秋时鲁国地名，又写作“陬”，在今山东曲阜附近。“鄹人之子”指孔子。
⑥ 皮：皮，用兽皮做成的箭靶子。
⑦ 科：等级。

Notes

1 resplendent [ri'splendənt] *a.* 光辉的
2 previous ['pri:viəs] *a.* 以前的
3 dynasty ['dainəsti] *n.* 王朝
4 Chou 周朝
5 the Grand Temple *n.* 太庙
6 remark [ri'mɑ:k] *v.* 说，谈论
7 Tsou 陬，在今山东曲阜附近
8 rite [rait] *n.* 仪式，礼制
9 pierce [piəs] *v.* 穿透

17. Tzu-kung wanted to do away with the sacrificial sheep at the ***announcement***[1] of the new moon. The Master said, 'Ssu, you are ***loath***[2] to part with the price of the sheep, but I am loath to see the ***disappearance***[3] of the rite.'

18. The Master said, 'You will be looked upon as obsequious by others if you observe every detail of the rites in serving your lord.'

19. Duke Ting asked, 'What is the way the ruler should employ the services of his ***subjects***[4]? What is the way a subject should serve his ruler?'

Confucius answered, 'The ruler should employ the services of his subjects ***in accordance with***[5] the rites. A subject should serve his ruler by doing his best.'

20. The Master said, 'In the ***kuan chü***[6*] there is joy without ***wantonness***[7], and sorrow without self-injury.'

---

* The first ode in the *Odes*.

17. 子贡欲去告朔[①]之饩羊[②]。子曰："赐也！尔爱[③]其羊，我爱其礼。"

子贡想要取消每月初一祭祀时用的活羊。孔子知道后说："赐啊！你舍不得你的羊，但我舍不得的是我的礼呀！"

18. 子曰："事君尽礼，人以为谄也。"

孔子说："侍奉君王时一切都按照礼制的要求去做，别人却以为是在向君主献媚。"

19. 定公[④]问："君使臣，臣事君，如之何？"孔子对曰："君使臣以礼，臣事君以忠。"

鲁定公问孔子："君主役使臣子，臣子侍奉君主，都应该怎样去做啊？"孔子回答道："君王让臣子做事应该以礼待臣；臣子应以忠心报君，全心侍奉君主。"

20. 子曰："《关雎》[⑤]，乐而不淫，哀而不伤。"

孔子说："《关雎》这首诗，快乐而不放荡，悲哀而不痛苦。"

Notes

1 announcement [ə'naunsmənt] *n.* 宣告

2 loath [ləuθ] *a.* 不愿意的，不舍得的

3 disappearance [ˌdisə'piərəns] *n.* 消失

4 subject ['sʌbdʒikt] *n.* 臣子

5 in accordance with 依照，与…一致

6 *kuan chü*《关雎》

7 wantonness ['wɔntənis] *n.* 放纵，淫荡

---

① 告朔：朔，农历每月初一为朔日。告朔，古代制度，天子每年秋冬之际，把第二年的历书颁发给诸侯，告知每个月的初一日。

② 饩羊：饩，音 xì。饩羊，祭祀用的活羊。

③ 爱：爱惜，舍不得的意思。

④ 定公：鲁国国君，姓姬名宋，定是谥号。公元前 509 ～公元前 495 年在位。

⑤ 《关雎》：雎，音 jū。这是《诗经》的第一篇。此篇写一君子"追求"淑女，思念时辗转反侧，寤寐思之的忧思，以及结婚时钟鼓乐之琴瑟友之的欢乐。

21. Duke Ai asked Tsai Wo about the ***altar***[1] to the god of earth. Tsai Wo replied, 'The Hsia used the ***pine***[2], the Yin used the ***cedar***[3], and the men of Chou used the ***chestnut***[4] *(li)*, saying that it made the common people ***tremble***[5] *(li)*.'

The Master, on hearing of this reply, commented, 'One does not explain away what is already done, one does not argue against what is already accomplished, and one does not condemn what has already gone by.'

22. The Master said, 'Kuan Chung was, indeed, a vessel of small ***capacity***[6].'

Someone remarked, 'Was Kuan Chung frugal, then?'

'Kuan Chung kept three separate establishments, each complete with its own staff. How can he be called frugal?'

'In that case, did Kuan Chung understand the rites?'

'Rulers of states ***erect***[7] ***gate-screens***[8]; ***Kuan Chung***[9] erected such a screen as well. The ruler of a state, when entertaining the ruler of another state, has a stand for ***inverted***[10] cups; Kuan Chung had such a stand as well. If even Kuan Chung understood the rites, who does not understand them.'

Notes

1 altar [ˈɔ:ltə] *n.* 圣坛，神主
2 pine [pain] *n.* 松树
3 cedar [ˈsi:də] *n.* 柏树
4 chestnut [ˈtʃesnʌt] *n.* 栗树
5 tremble [ˈtrembl] *v.* 发抖，战栗
6 capacity [kəˈpæsiti] *n.* 容纳…的能力
7 erect [iˈrekt] *v.* 建立
8 gate-screen *n.* 照壁
9 Kuan Chung 管仲
10 inverted [inˈvə:tid] *a.* 反向的，倒置的

21. 哀公问社① 于宰我，宰我② 对曰："夏后氏以松，殷人以柏，周人以栗，曰：使民战栗③。"子闻之，曰："成事不说，遂事不谏，既往不咎。"

鲁哀公问宰我，土地神的神社应该用什么树木制作，宰我说："夏代用松树，殷代用柏树，周代用栗树，取其'让民众恐惧、发抖'之意。"孔子听说后说："已经做过的事就不用提了，已经完成的事就不用再去劝阻了，已经过去的事也就不必再追究了。"

22. 子曰："管仲④ 之器小哉！"或曰："管仲俭乎？"曰："管氏有三归⑤，官事不摄⑥，焉得俭？""然则管仲知礼乎？"曰："邦君树塞门，管氏亦树塞门⑦；邦君为两君之好有反坫⑧，管氏亦有反坫。管氏而知礼，孰不知礼？"

孔子说："管仲的器量还是太小了呀！"有人问："管仲节俭吗？"孔子说："管仲收取人民大量市租，他家里的管事也是一人一职而不兼任，这怎么会是节俭呢？"有人又问："那么

---

① 社：土地神，祭祀土神的庙也称社。
② 宰我：名予，字子我，孔子的学生。
③ 战栗：恐惧，发抖。
④ 管仲：姓管名夷吾，齐国人，春秋时期的法家先驱。齐桓公的宰相，辅助齐桓公成为诸侯的霸主，公元前645年死。
⑤ 三归：相传是三处藏钱币的府库。
⑥ 摄：兼任。
⑦ 树塞门：树，树立。塞门，在大门口筑的一道短墙，以别内外，相当于屏风、照壁等。
⑧ 反坫：坫，音diàn。古代君主招待别国国君时，放置献过酒的空杯子的土台。

23. The Master talked of music to the Grand Musician of Lu, saying, 'This much can be known about music. It begins with playing in ***unison***[1]. When it gets into full swing, it is ***harmonious***[2], clear and unbroken. In this way it reaches the conclusion.'

24. The ***border***[3] official of Yi ***requested***[4] an audience, saying, 'I have never been denied an audience by any gentleman who has come to this place.' The followers presented him. When he came out, he said, 'What worry have you, gentlemen, about the loss of office? The Empire has long been without the Way. ***Heaven***[5] is about to use your Master as the ***wooden***[6] tongue for a bell.'[*]

---

* To rouse the Empire.

Notes

1 unison [ˈjuːnisən]
n. 一致；谐音

2 harmonious [hɑːˈməuniəs]
a. 和谐的

3 border [ˈbɔːdə]
n. 边疆

4 request [riˈkwest]
v. 请求

5 Heaven [ˈhevən]
n. 上天

6 wooden [ˈwudən]
a. 木制的

管仲懂得礼制吗？”孔子回答说：“齐君在大门口筑了一道照壁，管仲也在大门口筑一道照壁；齐君为招待别国国君而设置用来放置献过酒的空杯子的台子，管仲也设置一个。如果说管仲知道礼制，那还有谁是不知礼的呢？”

23. 子语①鲁大师②乐，曰：“乐其可知也：始作，翕③如也；从④之，纯⑤如也，皦⑥如也，绎⑦如也，以成。”

孔子告诉鲁太师演奏音乐的道理：“音乐的演奏是有规律的。刚开始演奏时，各种乐音和谐地配合，轻轻舒展开，慢慢发声；继续展开，音乐由小而大，悠扬悦耳，音节分明；到了高潮，或激昂慷慨或庄严肃穆，最后乐曲演奏完了，仍余音缭绕，后面好像还有悠悠未尽之意。”

24. 仪封人⑧请见，曰：“君子之至于斯也，吾未尝不得见也。”从者见之⑨。出，曰：“二三子何患于丧⑩乎？天下之无道也久矣，天将以夫子为木铎⑪。”

---

① 语：音 yù，告诉，动词用法。
② 大师：大，音 tài。大师是乐官名。
③ 翕：音 xī。意为合、聚、协调。
④ 从：音 zòng，意为放纵、展开。
⑤ 纯：美好、和谐。
⑥ 皦：音 jiǎo，音节分明。
⑦ 绎：连续不断。
⑧ 仪封人：仪为地名，在今河南兰考县境内。封人，系镇守边疆的官。
⑨ 从者见之：随行的人见了他。
⑩ 丧：失去，这里指失去官职。
⑪ 木铎：木舌的铜铃。古代天子发布政令时摇它以召集听众。

25. The Master said of the ***shao***[1*] that it was both perfectly beautiful and perfectly good, and of the ***wu***[2†] that it was perfectly beautiful but not perfectly good.

26. The Master said, 'What can I find worthy of note in a man who is lacking in tolerance when in high ***position***[3], in reverence when ***performing***[4] the rites and in ***sorrow***[5] when in mourning?'

---

* The music of Shun who came to the throne through the abdication of Yao.

† The music of King Wu who came to the throne through overthrowing the Yin by military force.

Notes

1 *shao*《韶》

2 *wu*《武》

3 position [pə'ziʃən] *n.* 职位

4 perform [pə'fɔ:m] *v.* 进行，完成

5 sorrow ['sɔrəu] *n.* 悲痛

仪地镇守边疆的官员请求拜见孔子，他说："凡是来到这里的有德行的人，没有一个是我不能见到的。"于是孔子的学生请求孔子接见他。官员拜见完孔子后对学生说："你们这些人担心失去官职干什么呢？天下文化礼制的丧失已经很久了，上天让孔子降生，就是想以他来警醒世人啊！"

25. 子谓《韶》①："尽美② 矣，又尽善③ 也。"谓《武》④："尽美矣，未尽善也。"

孔子谈论到《韶》乐的时候说："这支乐舞的音调、舞蹈美极了，表现的思想也善极了。当谈到《武》乐的时候则说：这支乐舞美极了，但还没做到善极。"

26. 子曰："居上不宽，为礼不敬，临丧不哀，吾何以观之哉？"

孔子说："居于统治地位而不宽以待人，行礼的时候也不庄严肃穆，对待丧事不真心哀戚，这种样子我怎么能看得下去呢？"

---

① 《韶》：相传是古代歌颂虞舜的一种乐舞。
② 《美》：指乐曲的音调、舞蹈的形式而言。
③ 《善》：指乐舞的思想内容而言的。
④ 《武》：相传是歌颂周武王的一种乐舞。

Book IV

1. The Master said, 'Of ***neighbourhoods***[1] benevolence is the most beautiful. How can the man be considered wise who, when he has the choice, does not settle in benevolence!?'

2. The Master said, 'One who is not benevolent cannot remain long in ***straitened***[2] ***circumstances***[3], nor can he remain long in easy circumstances.

'The benevolent man is attracted to benevolence because he feels at home in it. The wise man is attracted to benevolence because he finds it to his ***advantage***[4].'

卷　四

Notes

1 neighbourhood ['neibəhud] *n.* 邻居

2 straitened ['streitənd] *a.* 贫苦的

3 circumstance ['sə:kəmstəns] *n.* 环境

4 advantage [əd'vɑ:ntidʒ] *n.* 优势，利益

1. 子曰："里仁为美①，择不处仁②，焉得知③？"

孔子说："跟仁德的人做邻居才好，如果居住时不选择住在贤德的人的附近，我们又怎么能得到智慧呢？"

2. 子曰："不仁者不可以久处约④，不可以长处乐。仁者安仁⑤，知者利仁。"

孔子说："没有仁德之心的人不能长久地处在贫困中，也不能长久地处于安乐中。有仁德的人安于仁道，有智慧的人则是知道仁对自己有利才去实行仁道的。"

---

① 里仁为美：里，住处，借作动词用。住在有仁者的地方才好。

② 处：居住。

③ 知：音 zhì，同智。

④ 约：穷困、困窘。

⑤ 安仁、利仁：安仁是安于仁道；利仁，认为仁有利于自己才去行仁。

3. The Master said, 'It is only the benevolent man who is ***capable***[1] of liking or ***disliking***[2] other men.'

4. The Master said, 'If a man sets his heart on benevolence, he will be free from ***evil***[3].'

5. The Master said, 'Wealth and high station are what men desire but ***unless***[4] I got them in the right way I would not ***remain***[5] in them. ***Poverty***[6] and low station are what men dislike, but even if I did not get them in the right way I would not try to escape from them.*

'If the gentleman ***forsakes***[7] benevolence, in what way can he make a name for himself? The gentleman never ***deserts***[8] benevolence, not even for as long as it takes to eat a meal. If he hurries and ***stumbles***[9] one may be sure that it is in benevolence that he does so.'

6. The Master said, 'I have never met a man who finds benevolence attractive or a man who finds unbenevolence† ***repulsive***[10]. A man who finds benevolence attractive cannot be ***surpassed***[11]. A man who finds unbenevolence repulsive can, perhaps, be counted as benevolent, for he would not allow what is not benevolent to ***contaminate***[12] his person.

'Is there a man who, for the space of a single day, is able to devote all his ***strength***[13] to benevolence? I have not come across such a man whose strength proves ***insufficient***[14] for the task. There must be such cases of insufficient strength, only I have not come across them.'

---

* This sentence is most likely to be corrupt. The negative is probably an interpolation and the sentence should read: 'Poverty and low station are what men dislike, but if I got them in the right way I would not try to escape from them.'

† The word 'unbenevolence' has been coined because the original word has a positive meaning lacking in 'non-benevolence'.

Notes

1 capable [ˈkeipəbl] *a.* 有能力的

2 dislike [disˈlaik] *v.* 不喜欢，厌恶

3 evil [ˈiːvl] *n.* 邪恶

4 unless [ʌnˈles] *conj.* 除非，如果不

5 remain [riˈmein] *v.* 保持，留下

6 poverty [ˈpɔvəti] *n.* 贫穷

7 forsake [fəˈseik] *v.* 抛弃

8 desert [diˈzəːt] *v.* 离弃，背离

9 stumble [ˈstʌmbl] *v.* 绊倒，踌躇

10 repulsive [riˈpʌlsiv] *a.* 令人厌恶的

11 surpass [səˈpɑːs] *v.* 胜过

12 contaminate [kənˈtæmineit] *v.* 污染，使变坏

13 strength [streŋθ] *n.* 能力，力量

14 insufficient [ˌinsəˈfiʃənt] *a.* 不足的，不够的

3. 子曰："唯仁者能好[①]人，能恶[②]人。"

孔子说："唯有仁德的人能正确地喜欢一个人、厌恶一个人。"

4. 子曰："苟志于仁矣，无恶也。"

孔子说："如果立定志向实行仁道的话，总是没有坏处的。"

5. 子曰："富与贵，是人之所欲也，不以其道得之，不处也；贫与贱，是人之所恶也，不以其道得之，不去也。君子去仁，恶乎成名？君子无终食之间违仁，造次必于是，颠沛必于是。"

孔子说："财富与地位是每一个人所向往的，但不是以正当方式得到的，君子是不会接受的。贫穷与卑微是每个人所厌恶的，如果不是用正当的手段去改变这种境况，君子宁愿不改变。君子如果离开了仁德，又怎么能叫君子呢？君子不会在哪怕一顿饭的时间里背离仁德，即使在最紧迫的时刻也必须按照仁德办事，就是在颠沛流离的时候，也一定会按仁德去办事。"

6. 子曰："我未见好仁者，恶不仁者。好仁者，无以尚之；恶不仁者，其为仁矣，不使不仁者加乎其身。有能一日用其力于仁矣乎？我未见力不足者。盖有之矣，我未之见也。"

---

① 好：音 hào，喜爱的意思。作动词。

② 恶：音 wù，憎恶、讨厌。作动词。

7. The Master said, 'In his errors a man is true to ***type***[1]. Observe the errors and you will know the man.'

8. The Master said, 'He has not lived ***in vain***[2] who dies the day he is told about the Way.'

9. The Master said, 'There is no point in seeking the views of a Gentleman who, though he sets his heart on the Way, is ashamed of poor food and poor clothes.'

10. The Master said, 'In his dealings with the world the gentleman is not ***invariably***[3] for or against anything. He is on the side of what is moral.'

Notes

1 type [taip] *n.* 类型

2 in vain 无意义，徒劳

3 invariably [in'vɛəriəbli] *ad.* 不变地

孔子说："我没有见过爱好仁德的人，也没有见过厌恶不仁的人。爱好仁德的人，那是不能再好的了；厌恶不仁的人，在实行仁德的时候，只是不想让不仁德的人或事影响自己。有能每天都把自己的力量用在实行仁德上的人吗？我没有见过力量不够的（只是没有人去这样做罢了）。这种人大概也还是有的，但我没见过。"

7. 子曰："人之过也，各于其党。观过，斯知仁矣。"

孔子说："一个人会有过错，往往都是与他所处的各种社会关系有关。通过仔细考察这个人所犯的错误，就可以知道他是什么样的人了。"

8. 子曰："朝闻道，夕死可矣。"

孔子说："如果在早上听闻了真理，即使晚上就会死去，也没有什么遗憾了。"

9. 子曰："士志于道，而耻恶衣恶食者，未足与议也。"

孔子说："如果读书人立志要探求真理，却又对吃粗粮穿破衣的生活感到羞耻，这种人是不足以与他谈论人生至理的。"

10. 子曰："君子之于天下也，无适[①]也，无莫[②]也，义[③]之与比[④]。"

---

① 适：音 dí，意为亲近、厚待。

② 莫：疏远、冷淡。

③ 义：适宜、妥当。

④ 比：亲近、相近、靠近。

11. The Master said, 'While the gentleman ***cherishes***[1] ***benign***[2] rule, the small man cherishes his native land. While the gentleman cherishes a respect for the law, the small man cherishes generous treatment.'*

12. The Master said, 'If one is guided by profit in one's actions, one will ***incur***[3] much ill will.'

13. The Master said, 'If a man is able to govern a state by observing the rites and showing deference, what difficulties will he have in public life? If he is unable to ***govern***[4] a state by observing the rites and showing deference, what good are the rites to him?'

14. The Master said, 'Do not worry because you have no official position. Worry about your ***qualifications***[5]. Do not worry because no one appreciates your abilities. Seek to be worthy of appreciation.'

---

* The distinction here between 'the gentleman' and 'the small *man*' is not, as is often the case, drawn between the ruler and the ruled but within the class of the ruled.

Notes

1 cherish [ˈtʃeriʃ] *v.* 珍惜

2 benign [biˈnain] *a.* 仁慈的，宽厚的

3 incur [inˈkəː] *v.* 招致

4 govern [ˈɡʌvən] *v.* 统治，治理

5 qualification [ˌkwɔlifiˈkeiʃən] *n.* 资格，能力

孔子说："君子对于天下的人和事，没有固定的厚薄亲疏，只要合理恰当，便怎样做。"

11. 子曰："君子怀[①]德，小人怀土[②]；君子怀刑[③]，小人怀惠。"

孔子说："君子时刻不忘记德行，小人时刻惦记的只是乡土；君子关心法度，小人关心恩惠。"

12. 子曰："放[④]于利而行，多怨[⑤]。"

孔子说："只是为了追求利益而去做事，很容易招致别人的怨恨。"

13. 子曰："能以礼让为国乎，何有[⑥]？不能以礼让为国，如礼何[⑦]？"

孔子说："能够用礼让的原则来治理国家，那还有什么困难的呢？不能用礼让的原则来治理国家，怎么能实行礼制呢？"

14. 子曰："不患无位，患所以立；不患莫己知，求为可知也。"

孔子说："（君子）不担心没有地位，只担心自己没有学到得以安身立命的知识；不担心没有人知道自己，只求自己能成为有真才实学、值得为人们知道的人。"

---

① 怀：不忘记。
② 土：乡土。
③ 刑：法制惩罚。
④ 放：音 fǎng，同仿，效法，引申为追求。
⑤ 怨：别人的怨恨。
⑥ 何有：全意为"何难之有"，即不难的意思。
⑦ 如礼何：把礼怎么办？

15. The Master said, '***Ts'an***![1] There is one single thread ***binding***[2] my way together.'

Tseng Tzu ***assented***[3].

After the Master had gone out, the ***disciples***[4] asked, 'What did he mean?'

Tseng Tzu said, 'The way of the Master consists in doing one's best and in using oneself as a measure to ***gauge***[5] others. That is all.'

16. The Master said, 'The gentleman understands what is moral. The small man understands what is ***profitable***[6].'

17. The Master said, 'When you meet someone better than yourself, turn your thoughts to becoming his equal. When you meet someone not as good as you are, look within and examine your own self.'

18. The Master said, 'In serving your father and mother you ought to ***dissuade***[7] them from doing wrong in the gentlest way. If you see your advice being ***ignored***[8], you should not become ***disobedient***[9] but remain reverent. You should not complain even if in so doing you wear yourself out.'

15. 子曰：“参[①] 乎，吾道一以贯之。”曾子曰：“唯。”子出，门人问曰：“何谓也？”曾子曰：“夫子之道，忠恕[②] 而已矣。”

孔子说：“参呀，我的学说是由一个基本的思想贯彻始终的。”曾子说：“是的。”孔子出去以后，别的学生问曾子：“先生说的是什么意思呀？”曾子说：“老师的学说，主要是讲忠和恕罢了。”

16. 子曰：“君子喻于义，小人喻于利[③] 。”

孔子说：“君子明白的是义，小人只知道利。”

17. 子曰：“见贤思齐焉，见不贤而内自省[④] 也。”

孔子说：“看见贤德的人，就要努力学习向他靠齐，看见不贤德的人，就要立即反省自己有没有类似的缺点。”

18. 子曰：“事父母几[⑤] 谏，见志不从，又敬不违，劳[⑥] 而不怨。”

孔子说：“侍奉父母，（当他们有错的时候）要婉转地进行劝谏，如果他们不听从自己的意见，那也要态度恭敬而不要忤逆违背他们的意

Notes

1 Ts‘an 参，曾参，孔子的学生

2 bind [baind] *v.* 束缚，约束；结合

3 assent [əˈsent] *v.* 同意

4 disciple [diˈsaipl] *n.* 弟子

5 gauge [geidʒ] *v.* 衡量

6 profitable [ˈprɔfitəbl] *a.* 有利的

7 dissuade [diˈsweid] *v.* 劝说

8 ignore [igˈnɔː] *v.* 不理会，忽视

9 disobedient [ˌdisəˈbiːdiənt] *a.* 不顺从的

---

① 参：曾参，又称曾子，孔子的学生。

② 忠恕：忠是“己欲立而立人，己欲达而达人”，也就是忠诚待人。恕是“己所不欲，勿施于人”，也就是推己及人。

③ 义，利：此句中的“义”主要指伦理道德，比“正义”的含义广泛些。孔子这句话引起后世持续的“义利之辩”。

④ 内自省：检查自己有没有类似的缺点。

⑤ 几：音 jī，轻微、婉转的意思。

⑥ 劳：忧愁、烦劳的意思。

19. The Master said, 'While your parents are alive, you should not go too far ***afield***[1] in your travels. If you do, your ***whereabouts***[2] should always be known.'

20. The Master said, 'If, for three years, a man makes no changes to his father's ways, he can be said to be a good son.'

21. The Master said, 'A man should not be ***ignorant***[3] of the age of his father and mother. It is a matter, on the one hand, for ***rejoicing***[4] and, on the other, for anxiety.'

22. The Master said, 'In ***antiquity***[5] men were loath to speak. This was because they counted it shameful if their person failed to keep up with their words.'

23. The Master said, 'It is rare for a man to miss the mark through holding on to ***essentials***[6].'

愿，要为他们担忧操劳而不要心存怨恨。”

19. 子曰：“父母在，不远游[①]，游必有方[②]。”

孔子说：“父母在世的时候，不要离开他们去很远的地方，（避免他们没有人照顾）不得已而出外时，必须要告诉他们要去的地方。”

20. 子曰：“三年无改于父之道，可谓孝矣。”

孔子说：“如果过了很长一段时间，儿子都没有改变父亲在世时的好的作为，就可以说他是很孝顺的了。”

21. 子曰：“父母之年，不可不知也。一则以喜，一则以惧。”

孔子说：“父母的生日是不可以不知道的。一方面可以为他们的长寿而开心，另一方面也要为他们的年老而担忧。”

22. 子曰：“古者言之不出，耻躬之不逮也。”

孔子说：“古代的人，言语不轻易说出口，因为他们担心自己的行为会有做不到的地方。”

23. 子曰：“以约[③]失之者鲜[④]矣。”

孔子说：“时刻以礼制约束自己而又总犯错误的人，是很少见的呀。”

① 游：指游学、游宦、经商等外出活动。

② 方：一定的地方。

③ 约：约束。这里指“约之以礼”。

④ 鲜：少的意思。

Notes

1 afield [ə'fi:ld] *ad.* 远离地，向远方，在远方

2 whereabouts [ˌ(h)wɛərə'bauts] *n.* 所在之处

3 ignorant ['ignərənt] *a.* 无知的

4 rejoicing [ri'dʒɔisiŋ] *n.* 高兴，欣喜

5 antiquity [æn'tikwiti] *n.* 古代

6 essential [i'senʃəl] *n.* 本质，要点

24. The Master said, 'The gentleman desires to be ***halting***[1] in speech but quick in action.'

25. The Master said, 'Virtue never stands alone. It ***is bound to***[2] have neighbours.'

26. Tzu-yu said, 'To be ***importunate***[3] with one's lord will mean ***humiliation***[4]. To be importunate with one's friends will mean ***estrangement***[5].'

24. 子曰："君子欲讷① 于言而敏② 于行。"

孔子说："君子言语要谨慎，行动要勤敏。"

25. 子曰："德不孤，必有邻。"

孔子说："有道德的人是不会孤独的，一定会有志同道合的人来与他做伴。"

26. 子游曰："事君数③，斯④ 辱矣；朋友数，斯疏矣。"

子游说："侍奉君主过于烦琐，就会招致羞辱；对待朋友太过烦琐反而会导致疏远。"

Notes

1 halting [ˈhɔːltiŋ] *a.* 犹豫的

2 be bound to 必然，一定会

3 importunate [imˈpɔːtʃənit] *a.* 纠缠不休的

4 humiliation [hjuːˌmiliˈeiʃən] *n.* 耻辱，羞辱

5 estrangement [isˈtreindʒmənt] *n.* 疏远

① 讷：迟钝。这里指说话要谨慎。

② 敏：敏捷、快速的意思。

③ 数：音 shuò，屡次、多次，引申为烦琐的意思。

④ 斯：就。

Book V

1. The Master said of ***Kung-yeh Ch'ang***[1] that he was a suitable choice for a husband, for though he was in ***gaol***[2] it was not as though he had done anything wrong. He gave him his daughter in marriage.

2. The Master said of ***Nan-jung***[3] that when the Way ***prevailed***[4] in the state he was not cast aside and when the Way fell into ***disuse***[5] he stayed clear of the humiliation of punishment. He gave him his elder brother's daughter in marriage.

卷 五

Notes

1 Kung-yeh Ch'ang 公冶长，孔子的弟子

2 gaol [dʒeil] *n.* 监狱

3 Nan-jung 南容，孔子的学生

4 prevail [pri'veil] *v.* 盛行

5 disuse [dis'ju:s] *v.* 不用，废弃

1. 子谓公冶长①，“可妻也。虽在缧绁②之中，非其罪也。”以其子③妻之。”

孔子评论公冶长说：“（这个人）可以将女儿嫁给他。他虽然现在身陷监牢，但这并不是由于他的过错造成的。”于是就将自己的女儿嫁给了公冶长。

2. 子谓南容④：“邦有道⑤，不废⑥；邦无道，免于刑戮⑦。”以其兄之子妻之。

孔子评价南宫适说：“国家政治清明时，他是不会被埋没的；国家政治昏暗时，他也能善

---

① 公冶长：姓公冶名长，齐国人，孔子的弟子。

② 缧绁：音 léi xiè，捆绑犯人用的绳索，这里借指牢狱。

③ 子：古时无论儿、女均称子。

④ 南容：姓南宫名适（音 kuò），字子容。孔子的学生，通称他为南容。

⑤ 道：孔子这里所讲的道，是说国家的政治符合最高的和最好的原则。

⑥ 废：废置，不任用。

⑦ 刑戮：刑罚。

3. The Master's comment on Tzu-chien was 'What a gentleman this man is! If there were no gentlemen in Lu where could he have ***acquired***[1] his qualities?'

4. Tzu-kung asked, 'What do you think of me?' The Master said, 'You are a vessel.'

'What kind of vessel?'

'A sacrificial vessel.'*

5. Someone said, 'Yung is benevolent but does not have a ***facile***[2] tongue.'

The Master said, 'What need is there for him to have a facile tongue? For a man quick with a ***retort***[3] there are ***frequent***[4] occasions on which he will incur the ***hatred***[5] of others. I cannot say whether Yung is benevolent or not, but what need is there for him to have a facile tongue?'

---

* Made of jade.

Notes

1 acquire [ə'kwaiə] *v.* 获得

2 facile ['fæsəl] *a.* 熟练的，流畅的；口齿伶俐的

3 retort [ri'tɔ:t] *n.* 反驳

4 frequent ['fri:kwənt] *a.* 频繁的，惯常的

5 hatred ['heitrid] *n.* 憎恨，敌意

于自处，免去刑戮。”于是就将自己兄长的女儿嫁给南宫适。

3. 子谓子贱[①]，“君子哉若人[②]，鲁无君子者，斯焉取斯[③]。”

孔子评论子贱说：“这个人是君子呀！假若鲁国没有君子，那么这种人又是从哪里培养出这种好品德的呢？”

4. 子贡问曰：“赐也何如？”子曰：“女，器也。”曰：“何器也？”曰：“瑚琏[④] 也。”

子贡问孔子说：“我这个人怎么样啊？”孔子说：“你好比是一个器具。”子贡问道：“什么器具呀？”孔子回答道：“你就是宗庙里盛黍稷的瑚琏。”

5. 或曰：“雍[⑤] 也仁而不佞[⑥]。”子曰：“焉用佞？御人以口给[⑦]，屡憎于人，不知其仁[⑧]。焉用佞？”

有人评论冉雍说：“冉雍这个人很有仁德，但是没有口才。”孔子说：“要那么好的口才干什么呢？靠伶牙俐齿和人辩论，常常会招致别

---

① 子贱：姓宓（音 fú）名不齐，字子贱。生于公元前 521 年，比孔子小 49 岁。

② 若人：这个，此人。

③ 斯焉取斯：斯，此。第一个“斯”指子贱，第二个“斯”字指子贱的品德。

④ 瑚琏：古代祭祀时盛粮食用的器具。

⑤ 雍：姓冉名雍，字仲弓，生于公元前 522 年，孔子的学生。

⑥ 佞：音 nìng，能言善辩，有口才。

⑦ 口给：言语便捷、嘴快话多。

⑧ 不知其仁：指有口才者有仁与否不可知。

6. The Master told Ch'i-tiao K'ai to take office. Ch'i-tiao K'ai said, 'I cannot trust myself to do so yet.' The Master was pleased.

7. The Master said, 'If the Way should fail to prevail and I were to put to sea on a ***raft***[1], the one who would follow me would no doubt be Yu.' Tzu-lu, on hearing this, was ***overjoyed***[2]. The Master said, 'Yu has a greater love for ***courage***[3] than I, but is lacking in judgement.'

8. Meng Wu Po asked whether Tzu-lu was benevolent. The Master said, 'I cannot say.' Meng Wu Po repeated the question. The Master said, 'Yu can be given the responsibility of managing the military ***levies***[4] in a state of a thousand chariots, but whether he is benevolent or not I cannot say.'

'What about Ch'iu?'

人的厌恶，这样的人我不知道他是不是能做到有仁德。那么冉雍又何必一定要能言善辩呢？”

6. 子使漆雕开[①]仕。对曰："吾斯之未能信。"子说[②]。

孔子让漆雕开去做官。漆雕开说："我对做官这件事还没有信心。"孔子听后很高兴。

7. 子曰："道不行，乘桴[③]浮于海，从[④]我者，其由与！"子路闻之喜。子曰："由也好勇过我，无所取材。"

孔子说："如果我的主张最终不能实现，那我就会乘一个木筏子去海外了。跟随我的人恐怕只有仲由吧。"子路听说后非常高兴。孔子见了说道："仲由这个人太冲动鲁莽了，这种好勇的精神大大超过了我，这样的话做事就会不知道仲裁，不明断。"

8. 孟武伯问子路仁乎？子曰："不知也。"又问。子曰："由也，千乘之国，可使治其赋[⑤]也，不知其仁也。""求也何如？"子曰："求也，

Notes

1 raft [rɑːft] *n.* 木筏

2 overjoyed [ˌəuvəˈdʒɔid] *a.* 狂喜的

3 courage [ˈkʌridʒ] *n.* 勇气

4 levy [ˈlevi] *n.* 征税；征兵，所征的兵员

---

① 漆雕开：姓漆雕名开，字子开，一说字子若，生于公元前540年，孔子的门徒。

② 说：音 yuè，同"悦"。

③ 桴：音 fū，用来过河的木筏子。

④ 从：跟随、随从。

⑤ 赋：兵赋，向居民征收的军事费用。

The Master said, 'Ch'iu can be given the responsibility as a ***steward***[1] in a town with a thousand ***households***[2] or in a noble family with a hundred chariots, but whether he is benevolent or not I cannot say.'

'What about ***Ch'iu***[3]?'

The Master said, 'When Ch'iu, putting on his ***sash***[4], takes his place at court, he can be given the responsibility of ***conversing***[5] with the guests, but whether he is benevolent or not I cannot say.'

9. The Master said to Tzu-kung, 'Who is the better man, you or ***Hui***[6]?'

'How dare I compare myself with Hui? When he is told one

千室之邑[1]，百乘之家[2]，可使为之宰[3]也，不知其仁也。”“赤[4]也何如？”子曰：“赤也，束带立于朝[5]，可使与宾客[6]言也，不知其仁也。”

孟武伯问孔子子路算不算有仁德，孔子回答说：“不知道。”孟武伯又继续询问，孔子说：“仲由这个人啊，在有1,000乘马车的大国里，可以让他负责兵役和军政的工作。至于他有没有仁德，我不晓得。”

孟武伯又问：“冉求这个人怎么样呢？”孔子说：“冉求呢，在有千户人家的公邑或有百辆兵车的采邑里当总管是可以的。至于他有没有仁德，我不晓得。”

孟武伯问：“公西赤又怎么样呢？”孔子说：“公西赤嘛，可以让他穿着礼服，站在朝堂上接待贵宾，但我也不知道他是不是做到了仁。”

9. 子谓子贡曰：“女与回也孰愈[7]？”对曰：“赐也何敢望回？回也闻一以知十[8]，赐也闻一

① 千室之邑，邑是古代居民的聚居点，大致相当于后来的城镇。有1,000户人家的大邑。

② 百乘之家：指卿大夫的采地，当时大夫有车百乘，是采地中的较大者。

③ 宰：家臣、总管。

④ 赤：姓公西名赤，字子华，生于公元前509年，孔子的学生。

⑤ 束带立于朝：指穿着礼服立于朝廷。

⑥ 宾客：指一般客人和来宾。

⑦ 愈：胜过、超过。

⑧ 十：指数的全体，旧注云：“一，数之数；十，数之终。”

Notes

1 steward [stjuəd] *n.* 管家，主管

2 household ['haushəuld] *n.* 一家人，家庭，家事

3 Ch'iu 公西赤，字子华，孔子的学生

4 sash [sæʃ] *n.* 肩带

5 converse [kən'və:s] *v.* 交谈

6 Hui 颜回，孔子的学生

thing he understands ten. When I am told one thing I understand only two.'

The Master said, 'You are not as good as he is. Neither of us is as good as he is.'

10. Tsai Yü was in bed in the daytime. The Master said, 'A piece of ***rotten***[1] wood cannot be carved, nor can a wall of dried ***dung***[2] be ***trowelled***[3]. As far as Yü is concerned what is the use of ***condemning***[4] him.' The Master added, 'I used to take on trust a man's deeds after having listened to his words. Now having listened to a man's words I go on to observe his deeds. It was on account of Yü that I have changed in this respect.'

11. The Master said, 'I have never met anyone who is truly ***unbending***[5].'

Someone said, 'What about ***Shen Ch'eng***[6]?'

The Master said, 'Ch'eng is full of desires. How can he be unbending?'

Notes

1 rotten ['rɔtən] *a.* 腐烂的

2 dung [dʌŋ] *n.* 粪土

3 trowel ['trauəl] *v.* 用泥刀涂抹

4 condemn [kən'dem] *v.* 责难

5 unbending [ʌn'bendiŋ] *a.* 不屈的，坚定的

6 Shen Ch'eng 申枨，孔子的学生

以知二①。”子曰：“弗如也。吾与② 女弗如也。”

孔子对子贡说：“你和颜回哪一个人的学问更好一些呢？”子贡说：“我怎么可以和颜回相比呢？颜回听到一件事就可以推知 10 件事；而我知道一件事只能推知两件事。”孔子说：“是不如他呀，我同意你说的，是不如他。”

10. 宰予昼寝，子曰：“朽木不可雕也，粪土③之墙不可杇④ 也，于予与何诛⑤！”子曰：“始吾于人也，听其言而信其行；今吾于人也，听其言而观其行。于予与⑥改是。”

宰予大白天在屋里睡觉。孔子说：“腐烂了的木头没有办法在上面雕刻，腐土垒起的墙壁没有办法粉刷；至于宰予嘛，我又怎么能去责备他呢？”

孔子又说：“最开始的时候，我观察一个人，听到他所说的话，便相信他的行为；现在我观察一个人，会在听到他的话后，继续考察他的行为。由于宰予这件事以后，我才改变了态度的。”

11. 子曰：“吾未见刚者。”或对曰：“申枨⑦。”子曰：“枨也欲，焉得刚？”

---

① 二：旧注云：“二者，一之对也。”
② 与：赞同、同意。
③ 粪土：腐土、脏土。
④ 杇：音 wū，抹墙用的抹子。这里指用抹子粉刷墙壁。
⑤ 诛：意为责备、批评。
⑥ 与：语气词。
⑦ 申枨：枨，音 chéng。姓申名枨，字周，孔子的学生。

12. Tzu-kung said, 'While I do not wish others to ***impose***[1] on me, I also wish not to impose on others.'

The Master said, 'Ssu, that is quite beyond you.'

13. Tzu-kung said, 'One can get to hear about the Master's ***accomplishments***[2], but one cannot get to hear his views on human nature and the Way of Heaven.'

14. Before he could put into practice something he had heard, the only thing ***Tzu-lu***[3] feared was that he should be told something further.

15. Tzu-kung asked, 'Why was **K'ung Wen Tzu**[4] called "*wen*"?'

The Master said, 'He was quick and eager to learn: he was not ashamed to seek the advice of those who were ***beneath***[5] him in station. That is why he was called "wen".'

孔子说："我没有见过刚毅不屈的人。"有的人回答道："申枨就是呀。"孔子说："申枨做事情还是会存有一些欲望，这样的人又怎么会刚毅不屈呢？"

12. 子贡曰："我不欲人之加诸我也，吾亦欲无加诸人。"子曰："赐也，非尔所及也。"

子贡说："我不希望别人强加给我一些事，我也不会强加给别人事情。"孔子说："赐啊，这样的事你还做不到呢。"

13. 子贡曰："夫子之文章①，可得而闻也；夫子之言性② 与天道③，不可得而闻也。"

子贡说："先生在诗书礼乐等各方面的学问我们可以（在日常学习中）学到，先生关于天道命运方面的学识则是我们怎么学也学不到的。"

14. 子路有闻，未之能行，唯恐有闻。

子路听到一个道理，但没有能够亲自实行的时候，唯恐又听到新的道理。

15. 子贡问曰："孔文子④ 何以谓之文也？"子曰："敏⑤ 而好学，不耻下问，是以谓之文也。"

子贡问孔子："孔文子的谥号为什么是'文'

Notes

1 impose [im'pəuz] v. 强加

2 accomplishment [ə'kɔmpliʃmənt] n. 成就

3 Tzu-lu 子路

4 K'ung Wen Tzu 孔文子，卫国大夫孔圉

5 beneath [bi'ni:θ] prep. 在…之下

① 文章：这里指孔子传授的诗书礼乐等。

② 性：人性。

③ 天道：天命。《论语》书中孔子多处讲到天和命，但不见有孔子关于天道的言论。

④ 孔文子：卫国大夫孔圉（音 yǔ），"文"是谥号，"子"是尊称。

⑤ 敏：敏捷、勤勉。

16. The Master said of ***Tzu-ch'an***[1] that he had the way of the gentleman on four counts: he was respectful in the manner he conducted himself; he was reverent in the service of his lord; in caring for the common people, he was generous and, in employing their services, he was just.

17. The Master said, 'Yen P'ing-chung ***excelled***[2] in friendship: even after long ***acquaintance***[3] he treated his friends with reverence.'

18. The Master said, 'When housing his great ***tortoise***[4], ***Tsang Wen-chung***[5] had the capitals of the ***pillars***[6] carved in the shape of hills and the ***rafterposts***[7] painted in a ***duckweed***[8] design. What is one to think of his intelligence?'

Notes

1 Tzu-ch'an 子产，郑国大夫

2 excel [ik'sel] *v.* 优于，擅长

3 acquaintance [ə'kweintəns] *n.* 熟人，相识

4 tortoise ['tɔ:təs] *n.* 乌龟

5 Tsang Wen-chung 臧文仲

6 pillar ['pilə] *n.* 柱子

7 rafterpost ['ræftəpəust] *n.* 房梁上的短柱

8 duckweed ['dʌkwi:d] *n.* 浮萍

呢？”孔子说：“聪明勤勉而又刻苦学习，遇到不懂的问题，随时向人请教，而不在乎别人身份地位的高低，所以谥号为‘文’。”

16. 子谓子产① 有君子之道四焉：“其行己也恭，其事上也敬，其养民也惠，其使民也义。”

孔子评价子产有四种行为合于君子之道：“他自己的行为举止庄严肃穆，他对待君王恭敬有礼，他教导人民恩惠有加，他役使百姓合于义理法度。”

17. 子曰：“晏平仲② 善与人交，久而敬之③。”

孔子说：“晏平仲很会跟人交往，交往越久，别人对他越恭敬有礼。”

18. 子曰：“臧文仲④ 居蔡⑤，山节藻棁⑥，何如其知也！”

孔子说：“臧文仲养了一只大龟，龟室的斗拱雕成山的形状，短柱上画以水草花纹，他这个人又怎么能算是有智慧的人呢？”

---

① 子产：姓公孙名侨，字子产，郑国大夫，做过正卿，是郑穆公的孙子，为春秋时郑国的贤相。

② 晏平仲：齐国的贤大夫，名婴。《史记》第62卷有他的传。“平”是他的谥号。

③ 久而敬之：“之”在这里指代晏平仲。

④ 臧文仲：姓臧孙名辰，“文”是他的谥号。因不遵守周礼，被孔子指责为“不仁”“不智”。

⑤ 蔡：国君用以占卜的大龟。蔡这个地方产龟，所以把大龟叫做蔡。

⑥ 山节藻棁：节，柱上的斗拱。棁，音zhuō，房梁上的短柱。把斗拱雕成山形，在棁上绘以水草花纹。这是古时装饰天子宗庙的做法。

19. Tzu-chang asked, ***'Ling Yin*** [*] ***Tzu-wen*** [1] gave no appearance of pleasure when he was made prime minister three times. Neither did he give any appearance of displeasure when he was removed from office three times. He always told his ***successor*** [2] what he had done during his term of office. What do you think of this?'

The Master said, 'He can, indeed, be said to be a man who does his best.'

'Can he be said to be benevolent.'

'He cannot even be said to to be wise. How can he be said to be benevolent?'

'When ***Ts'ui Tzu*** [3] ***assassinated*** [4] the Lord of Ch'i, ***Ch'en Wen Tzu*** [5] who owned ten teams of four horses each ***abandoned*** [6] them and left the state. On arriving in another state, he said, "The officials here are no better than our ***Counsellor*** [7] Ts'ui Tzu." He left and went to yet another state. Once more, he said, "The officials here are no better than our Counsellor Ts'ui Tzu," and he again left. What do you think of this?'

The Master said, 'He can, indeed, be said to be pure.'

'Can he be said to be benevolent.'

'He cannot even be said to be wise. How can he be said to be benevolent?'

---

* This was the title in the state of Ch'u for the prime minister.

Notes

1 Ling Yin Tzu-wen 令尹子文，楚国宰相；令尹，楚国官名

2 successor [sək'sesə] *n.* 后继者

3 Ts'ui Tzu 崔杼，齐国大夫

4 assassinate [ə'sæsineit] *v.* 暗杀

5 Ch'en Wen Tzu 陈文子，陈国大夫

6 abandon [ə'bændən] *v.* 放弃

7 counsellor ['kaunsələ] *n.* 大臣

19. 子张问曰："令尹子文①三仕为令尹，无喜色；三已②之，无愠色。旧令尹之政，必以告新令尹。何如？"子曰："忠矣。"曰："仁矣乎？"曰："未知。焉得仁？""崔子③弑④齐君⑤，陈子文⑥有马十乘，弃而违之，至于他邦，则曰：'犹吾大夫崔子也。'违之。之一邦，则又曰：'犹吾大夫崔子也。'违之，何如？子曰："清矣。"曰："仁矣乎？"曰："未知，焉得仁？"

子张问孔子说："楚国的令尹子文几次做楚国宰相，没有显出高兴的样子，几次被免职，也没有显出怨恨的样子；他每次被免职时，一定把以前的政务都告诉来接任的新宰相。这个人怎么样啊？"孔子说："可算尽忠于国家了。"子张问："算得上仁了吗？"孔子说："不知道。这怎么能算仁呢？"

子张又问："崔杼杀了他的君主齐庄公，陈文子家很富有，有40匹马，都舍弃不要而离开了齐国，到了另一个国家，他说，这里的执政者也和我们齐国的大夫崔杼差不多，于是就离开了。到了另一个国家，又说，这里的执政者也和我们的大夫崔杼差不多，又离开了。这

① 令尹子文：令尹，楚国的官名，相当于宰相。子文是楚国的著名宰相。

② 三已：三，指多次。已，罢免。

③ 崔文：齐国大夫崔杼（音 zhù）曾杀死齐庄公，在当时引起极大反应。

④ 弑：地位在下的人杀了地位在上的人。

⑤ 齐君：即指被崔杼所杀的齐庄公。

⑥ 陈文子：陈国的大夫，名须无。

20. Chi Wen Tzu always thought three times before taking action. When the Master was told of this, he commented, 'Twice is quite enough.'

21. The Master said, 'Ning Wu Tzu was intelligent when the Way prevailed in the state, but stupid when it did not. Others may equal his intelligence but they cannot equal his ***stupidity***[1].'

22. When he was in Ch'en, the Master said, 'Let us go home. Let us go home. Our young men at home are wildly ***ambitious***[2]**,** and have great accomplishments for all to see, but they do not know how to ***prune***[3] themselves.'

个人你看怎么样？”孔子说：“可以算得上清高了。”子张说：“这算不算仁呢？”孔子说：“不知道。这怎么能算得上仁呢？”

20. 季文子① 三思而后行。子闻之，曰：“再，斯② 可矣。”

季文子每做一件事都要考虑很多次才行动。孔子听说后，说：“想两次就可以了。”

21. 子曰：“宁武子③，邦有道则知，邦无道则愚④，其知可及也，其愚不可及也。”

孔子说：“宁武子这个人，在国家太平时节他就显得聪明，当国家无道昏暗时，他就装傻。他的那种聪明别人可以做得到，他那种装傻别人就做不到了。”

22. 子在陈⑤ 曰：“归与！归与！吾党之小子⑥ 狂简⑦，斐然⑧ 成章，不知所以裁⑨ 之。”

孔子在陈国，说：“回去吧！回去吧！我们家乡的学生有远大志向，但行为粗率简单；文采斐然可观，但还不知道怎样来约束自己。”

Notes

1 stupidity [stuːˈpiditi] *n.* 愚蠢

2 ambitious [æmˈbiʃəs] *a.* 有野心的

3 prune [pruːn] *v.* 修整；约束

---

① 季文子：即季孙行父，鲁成公、鲁襄公时任正卿，“文”是他的谥号。

② 斯：就。

③ 宁武子：姓宁名俞，卫国大夫，“武”是他的谥号。

④ 愚：这里是装傻的意思。

⑤ 陈：古国名，大约在今河南东部和安徽北部一带。

⑥ 吾党之小子：古代以 500 家一为党。吾党意即我的故乡。小子，指孔子在鲁国的学生。

⑦ 狂简：志向远大但行为粗率简单。

⑧ 斐然：斐，音 fěi，有文采的样子。

⑨ 裁：裁剪，节制。

23. The Master said, '***Po Yi***[1] and ***Shu Ch'i***[2] never remembered old scores. For this reason they incurred little ill will.'

24. The Master said, 'Who said ***Wei-sheng Kao***[3] was straight? Once when someone begged him for ***vinegar***[4], he went and begged it off a neighbour to give it to him.'

25. The Master said, 'Cunning words, an ingratiating face and ***utter***[5] ***servility***[6], these things ***Tso-ch'iu Ming***[7] found shameful. I, too, find them shameful. To be friendly towards someone while ***concealing***[8] one's ***hostility***[9], this Tso-ch'iu Ming found shameful. I, too, find it shameful.'

Notes

1 Po Yi 伯夷，孤竹军的儿子

2 Shu Ch'i 叔齐，孤竹军的儿子

3 Wei-sheng Kao 微生高，当时人认为他直率

4 vinegar ['vinigə] *n.* 醋

5 utter ['ʌtə] *a.* 完全的，十足的

6 servility [səː'viliti] *n.* 奴性，卑屈

7 Tso-ch'iu Ming 左丘明，鲁国人

8 conceal [kən'siːl] *v.* 隐藏

9 hostility [hɔs'tiliti] *n.* 敌意

23. 子曰："伯夷叔齐① 不念旧恶②，怨是用希③。"

孔子说："伯夷、叔齐这两兄弟不记念过去的仇恨，因此别人对他们的怨恨也就很少。"

24. 子曰："孰谓微生高④ 直？或乞醯⑤ 焉，乞诸其邻而与之。"

孔子说："谁说微生高这个人直率？有人向他借点醋，他不直说自己没有，却跑到邻居家里讨了点转借给人。"

25. 子曰："巧言令色足恭⑥，左丘明⑦ 耻之，丘亦耻之。匿怨而友其人，左丘明耻之，丘亦耻之。"

孔子说："花言巧语、伪善的脸色、逢迎的姿态、低三下四的恭顺，这种态度，左丘明认为可耻，我也认为可耻。内心怀有怨恨，表面上却装出友好的样子，这种行为，左丘明认为可耻，我也认为可耻。"

---

① 伯夷、叔齐：殷朝末年孤竹君的两个儿子。父亲死后，二人互相让位，都逃到周文王那里。周武王起兵伐纣，他们认为这是以臣弑君，是不忠不孝的行为，曾加以拦阻。周灭商统一天下后，他们以吃周朝的粮食为耻，逃进深山中以野草充饥，饿死在首阳山中。

② 恶：嫌隙，仇恨。

③ 希：同稀。

④ 微生高：姓微生名高，鲁国人。当时人认为他为直率。

⑤ 醯：音 xī，即醋。

⑥ 足恭：一说是两只脚做出恭敬逢迎的姿态来讨好别人；另一说是过分恭敬。这里采用后说。

⑦ 左丘明：姓左丘名明，鲁国人，相传是《左传》一书的作者。

26. ***Yen Yüan***[1] and ***Chi-lu***[2] were in attendance. The Master said, 'I suggest you each tell me what it is you have set your hearts on.'

Tzu-lu said, 'I should like to share my ***carriage***[3] and horses, clothes and furs with my friends, and to have no regrets even if they become worn.'

Yen Yüan said, 'I should like never to ***boast***[4] of my own goodness and never to impose ***onerous***[5] tasks upon others.'

Tzu-lu said, 'I should like to hear what you have set your heart on.'

The Master said, 'To bring peace to the old, to have trust in my friends, and to cherish the young.'

27. The Master said, 'I suppose I should give up hope. I have yet to meet the man who, on seeing his own errors, is able to take himself to task ***inwardly***[6].'

28. The Master said, 'In a ***hamlet***[7] of ten households, there are bound to be those who are my equal in doing their best for others and in being trustworthy in what they say, but they are unlikely to be as eager to learn as I am.'

Notes

1 Yen Yüan 颜渊

2 Chi-lu 季路，又字子路

3 carriage [ˈkæridʒ] *n.* 马车

4 boast [bəust] *v.* 吹嘘

5 onerous [ˈɔnərəs] *a.* 繁重的

6 inwardly [ˈinwədli] *ad.* 在心里

7 hamlet [ˈhæmlit] *n.* 小村子

26. 颜渊、季路侍①。子曰："盍②各言尔志。"子路曰："原车马，衣轻裘，与朋友共，敝之而无憾。"颜渊曰："愿无伐③善，无施劳④。"子路曰："愿闻子之志。"子曰："老者安之，朋友信之，少者怀之⑤。"

颜渊、子路两人侍立在孔子身边。孔子说："何不各人说说自己的志向？"子路说："愿意把我的车马、衣服、皮袍与朋友共同使用，即使用坏了也不抱怨。"颜渊说："我愿意不夸耀自己的长处，不表白自己的功劳。"子路向孔子说："希望听听您的志向。"孔子说："我的志向是让年长者生活安逸，让朋友们信任我，让年轻的子弟们得到关怀。"

27. 子曰："已矣乎！吾未见能见其过而内自讼者也。"

孔子说："算了吧，我还从来没见过能够看到自己的错误便能从内心责备自己的人。"

28. 子曰："十室之邑，必有忠信如丘者焉，不如丘之好学也。"

孔子说："就是在只有10户人家的小村子，也一定会有像我这样讲忠信的人，只是不如我那样好学罢了。"

---

① 侍：服侍，站在旁边陪着尊贵者叫侍。

② 盍：何不。

③ 伐：夸耀。

④ 施劳：施，表白。劳，功劳。

⑤ 少者怀之：让少者得到关怀。

Book VI

1. The Master said, 'Tung could be given the seat facing south.'*

2. ***Chung-kung***[1] asked about ***Tzu-sang Po-tzu***[2]. The Master said, 'It is his ***simplicity***[3] of style that makes him acceptable.'

Chung-kung said, 'In ruling over the common people, is it not acceptable to hold oneself in reverence and merely to be simple in the measures one takes? On the other hand, is it not carrying simplicity too far to be simple in the way one holds oneself as well as in the measures one takes?'

The Master said, 'Yung is right in what he says.'

---

* The seat of the ruler.

卷　六

Notes

1 Chung-kung 仲弓

2 Tzu-sang Po-tzu 桑伯子

3 simplicity [sim'plisiti] *n.* 简单

1. 子曰："雍也可使南面。"

孔子说："冉雍这个人，可以让他去做（某一方面的）长官。"

2. 仲弓问子桑伯子①。子曰："可也，简②。"仲弓曰："居敬③而行简④，以临⑤其民，不亦可乎？居简而行简，无乃⑥大⑦简乎？"子曰："雍之言然。"

仲弓向孔子询问桑伯子这个人。孔子说："这个人还可以，可以用'简单、豁达'来评价。"仲弓又问："如果依礼严格要求自己，做事简明扼要，用这种方式来为百姓处理事务，不也可

① 桑伯子：人名，此人生平不可考。
② 简：简要，不烦琐。
③ 居敬：为人严肃认真，依礼严格要求自己。
④ 行简：指推行政事简而不繁。
⑤ 临：面临、面对。此处有"治理"的意思。
⑥ 无乃：岂不是。
⑦ 大：同"太"。

3. When Duke Ai asked which of his disciples was eager to learn, Confucius answered, 'There was one Yen Hui who was eager to learn. He did not ***vent***[1] his anger upon an ***innocent***[2] person, nor did he make the same mistake twice. ***Unfortunately***[3] his ***allotted***[4] span was a short one and he died. Now there is no one. No one eager to learn has come to my notice.'

4. ***Jan Tzu***[5] asked for grain for the mother of ***Tzu-hua***[6] who was away on a ***mission***[7] to Ch'i. The Master said, 'Give her one fu.'* Jan Tzu asked for more. 'Give her one *yü*.' Jan Tzu gave her five ***ping***[8] of grain.

The Master said, 'Ch'iu went off to Ch'i drawn by well-fed horses and wearing light furs. I have heard it said, A gentleman gives to help the ***needy***[9] and not to ***maintain***[10] the rich in style.'

---

* *Fu*, *yü* and *ping* are dry measures in ascending order of capacity.

以吗？而如果用只求简单、少找麻烦的态度简单处理政务，不是太不负责任了吗？”孔子听了说：“冉雍，你说得很对啊。”

3. 哀公问：“弟子孰为好学？”孔子对曰：“有颜回者好学，不迁怒[①]，不贰过[②]，不幸短命死矣[③]。今也则亡[④]，未闻好学者也。”

鲁哀公问孔子：“你的学生里面哪一个最好学呀？”孔子回答说：“有一个叫颜回的学生很好学，他从不迁怒于别人，也从不重犯同样的过错。但很不幸，他很早就死了。现在学生里已经没有这样的人了，没有听说谁好学。”

4. 子华[⑤]使于齐，冉子[⑥]为其母请粟[⑦]。子曰：“与之釜[⑧]。”请益。曰：“与之庾[⑨]。”冉子与之粟五秉[⑩]。子曰：“赤之适齐也，乘肥马，衣

---

① 不迁怒：不把对此人的怒气发泄到彼人身上。

② 不贰过：“贰”是重复、一再的意思。这是说不犯同样的错误。

③ 短命死矣：颜回死时年仅 31 岁。

④ 亡：同“无”。

⑤ 子华：姓公西名赤，字子华，孔子的学生，比孔子小 42 岁。

⑥ 冉子：冉有，在《论语》书中被孔子弟子称为“子”的只有四五个人，冉有即其中之一。

⑦ 粟：在古文中，粟与米连用时，粟指带壳的谷粒，去壳以后叫做米；粟字单用时，就是指米了。

⑧ 釜：音 fǔ，古代计量单位，1 釜约等于 6 斗 4 升。

⑨ 庾：音 yǔ，古代计量单位，1 庾等于 2 斗 4 升。

⑩ 秉：音丙，bǐng，古代计量单位，16 斛。5 秉则是 80 斛。古代以 10 斗为斛。南宋贾似道时才改为 5 斗 1 斛，1 石 2 斛，沿用到民国初年，这一计量单位现已废除。周秦的 80 斛合今天的 16 石。

Notes

1 vent [vent] *v.* 发泄

2 innocent ['inəsənt] *a.* 无罪的，清白的

3 unfortunately [ʌn'fɔ:tʃənitli] *ad.* 不幸地

4 allotted [ə'lɔtid] *a.* 指定的，分配的

5 Jan Tzu 冉子，冉有

6 Tzu-hua 子华，孔子的学生

7 mission ['miʃən] *n.* 使命；任务

8 ping [piŋ] 秉，古代计量单位

9 needy ['ni:di] *a.* 穷困的

10 maintain [mein'tein] *v.* 维持，继续

5. On becoming his* steward, ***Yüan Ssu***[1] was given nine hundred measures of grain which he declined. The Master said, 'Can you not find a use for it in helping the people in your neighbourhood?'

6. The Master said of Chung-kung, 'Should a bull born of plough cattle have a ***sorrel***[2] coat and well-formed horns, would the ***spirits***[3] of the mountains and rivers allow it to be passed over even if we felt it was not good enough to be used?'

---

* i.e., Confucius'.

Notes

1 Yüan Ssu 原思，孔子的学生

2 sorrel ['sɔrəl] *a.* 红褐色的，栗色的

3 spirit ['spirit] *n.* 神

轻裘。吾闻之也：君子周① 急不济富。”

公西赤出使齐国，冉有替他的母亲向孔子请求补助一些谷米。孔子说：“给她一釜。”冉有请求再增加一些。孔子说：“再给她一庾。”冉有却给她五秉。孔子说：“公西赤去齐国，乘着骏马拉的车子，穿着暖和轻便的皮袍。我听说过，君子只是雪中送炭同济急需，而不是锦上添花为富人增富。”

5. 原思② 为之宰③，与之粟九百④，辞。子曰：“毋，以与尔邻里乡党⑤ 乎！”

原宪做孔子家的总管，孔子给他俸米九百，原宪推辞不要。孔子说：“你不要推辞。（如果有多的）给你的邻里（中需要它们的人）吧。”

6. 子谓仲弓，曰：“犁牛⑥ 之子骍且角⑦。虽欲勿用⑧，山川⑨ 其舍诸⑩？”

---

① 周：周济、救济。

② 原思：姓原名宪，字子思，鲁国人。孔子的学生，生于公元前 515 年。孔子在鲁国任司法官的时候，原思曾做他家的总管。

③ 宰：家宰，管家。

④ 九百：没有说明单位是什么。

⑤ 邻里乡党：相传古代以 5 家为邻，25 家为里，12,500 家为乡，500 家为党。此处指原思的同乡，或家乡周围的百姓。

⑥ 犁牛：即耕牛。古代祭祀用的牛不能以耕牛代替，系红毛长角，单独饲养的。

⑦ 骍且角：骍：音 xīn，红色。祭祀用的牛，毛色为红，角长得端正。

⑧ 用：用于祭祀。

⑨ 山川：山川之神。此喻上层统治者。

⑩ 其舍诸：其，有“怎么会”的意思。舍，舍弃。诸，“之于”二字的合音。

7. The Master said, 'In his heart for three months at a time Hui does not lapse from benevolence. The others ***attain***[1] benevolence merely by fits and starts.'

8. Chi K'ang Tzu asked, 'Is Chung Yu good enough to be given office?'

The Master said, 'Yu is ***resolute***[2]. What difficulties could there be for him in ***taking office***[3]?'

'Is Ssu good enough to be given office?'

'Ssu is a man of ***understanding***[4]. What difficulties could there be for him in taking office?'

'Is Ch'iu good enough to be given office?'

'Ch'iu is accomplished. What difficulties could there be for him in taking office?'

Notes

1 attain [ə'tein] *v.* 达到

2 resolute ['rezəluːt] *a.* 坚定的，果断的

3 take office 执政

4 understanding [ˌʌndə'stændiŋ] *n.* 理解，通达事理

孔子评价仲弓说："耕牛产下了长着红色的毛、端正的角的牛犊，人们虽然不想用它做祭品，但山川之神难道会舍弃它吗？"

7. 子曰："回也，其心三月① 不违仁，其余则日月② 至焉而已矣。"

孔子说："颜回这个人，他的心可以长久不离仁德，其余的学生则只能在短时间内做到或者想到仁罢了。"

8. 季康子③ 问："仲由可使从政也与？"子曰："由也果④，于从政乎何有？"曰："赐也可使从政也与？"曰："财也达⑤，于从政乎何有？"曰："求也可使从政也与？"曰："求也艺⑥，于从政乎何有？"

季康子问孔子："仲由这个人，可以让他管理国家政事吗？"孔子说："仲由做事果断，让他管理国家政事有什么困难呢？"季康子又问："端木赐这个人，可以让他管理国家政事吗？"孔子说："端木赐通达事理，他管理政事又能有什么困难呢？"季康子又问道："冉求这个人，可以让他管理国家政事吗？"孔子说："冉求多

---

① 三月：指较长的时间。

② 日月：指较短的时间。

③ 季康子：他在公元前 492 年继其父为鲁国正卿，此时孔子正在各地游说。8 年以后，孔子返回鲁国，冉求正在帮助季康子推行革新措施。孔子于是对此三人做出了评价。

④ 果：果断、决断。

⑤ 达：通达、顺畅。

⑥ 艺：有才能技艺。

9. The Chi Family wanted to make Min Tzu-ch'ien the steward of Pi. Min Tzu-ch'ien said, 'Decline the offer for me ***tactfully***[1]. If anyone comes back for me, I shall be on the other side of the River Wen.'*

10. ***Po-niu***[2] was ill. The Master visited him and, holding his hand through the window, said, 'We are going to lose him. It must be ***Destiny***[3]. Why else should such a man be ***stricken***[4] with such a disease? Why else should such a man be stricken with such a disease?'

11. The Master said, 'How ***admirable***[5] Hui is! Living in a mean dwelling on a ***bowlful***[6] of rice and a ***ladleful***[7] of water is a hardship most men would find intolerable, but Hui does not allow this to affect his joy. How admirable Hui is!'

---

* i.e., over the border into the state of Ch'i.

Notes

1 tactfully ['tæktfəli] *ad.* 机智地

2 Po-niu 伯牛，孔子的学生

3 Destiny ['destini] 命运

4 stricken ['strikən] *a.* 受伤或患病的

5 admirable ['ædmərəbl] *a.* 令人钦佩的，优秀的

6 bowlful ['bəulfəl] *n.* 一碗

7 ladleful ['leidlfəl] *n.* 一勺

才多艺，他对于管理国家政事有什么困难呢？”

9. 季氏使闵子骞① 为费② 宰，闵子骞曰：“善为我辞焉！如有复我③ 者，则吾必在汶上④ 矣。”

季氏派人请闵子骞做费邑的长官，闵子骞（对来请他的人）说：“请你替我好好地推辞掉吧！如果再来召我，那我一定会逃跑到汶水那边（的齐国）去的。”

10. 伯牛⑤ 有疾，子问之，自牖⑥ 执其手，曰：“亡之⑦，命矣夫⑧，斯人也而有斯疾也！斯人也而有斯疾也！”

冉耕生病了，孔子去探望他。孔子从窗户外面握着他的手说：“没办法呀，这大概是命里注定的吧！这样的人竟会得这样的病啊，这样的人竟会得这样的病啊！”

11. 子曰：“贤哉回也，一箪⑨ 食，一瓢饮，在陋巷⑩，人不堪其忧，回也不改其乐⑪。贤哉

---

① 闵子骞：姓闵名损，字子骞，鲁国人，孔子的学生，比孔子小 15 岁。

② 费：音 mì，季氏的封邑，在今山东费县西北一带。

③ 复我：再来召我。

④ 汶上：汶，音 wèn，水名，即今山东大汶河，当时流经齐、鲁两国之间。在汶上，是说要离开鲁国到齐国去。

⑤ 伯牛：姓冉名耕，字伯牛，鲁国人，孔子的学生。孔子认为他的“德行”较好。

⑥ 牖：音 yǒu，窗户。

⑦ 亡之：一作丧夫解，一作死亡解。

⑧ 夫：音 fú，语气词，相当于“吧”。

⑨ 箪：音 dān，古代盛饭用的竹器。

⑩ 巷：此处指颜回的住处。

⑪ 乐：乐于学。

12. Jan Ch'iu said, 'It is not that I am not pleased with your way, but rather that my strength gives out.' The Master said, 'A man whose strength gives out ***collapses***[1] along the course. In your case you set the limits ***beforehand***[2].'

13. The Master said to Tzu-hsia, 'Be a gentleman ***ju***[3], * not a ***petty***[4] ju.'

14. Tzu-yu was the steward of Wu Ch'eng. The Master said, 'Have you made any discoveries there?'

'There is one T'an-t'ai Mieh-ming who never takes ***short-cuts***[5] and who has never been to my room except on official business.'

---

* The original meaning of the word is uncertain, but it probably referred to men for whom the qualities of the scholar were more important than those of the warrior. In subsequent ages, *ju* came to be the name given to the Confucianists.

Notes

1 collapse [kə'læps] *v.* 倒塌

2 beforehand [bi'fɔ:hænd] *ad.* 提前地，预先

3 ju 儒

4 petty ['peti] *a.* 小的；小人的，卑劣的

5 short-cut ['ʃɔ:tkʌt] *n.* 捷径

回也。”

孔子说：“颜回的品德多么高尚啊！一竹篮饭、一瓢水，住在简陋的地方，别人都忍受不了这种穷苦的生活，颜回却没有改变他好学的天性。颜回的品德多么高尚啊！”

12. 冉求曰：“非不说[①]子之道，力不足也。”子曰：“力不足者，中道而废。今女画[②]。”

冉求说：“我不是不喜欢老师的学说，而是我的能力不够呀。”孔子说：“能力不够的话应该是走到半路才停下来，而现在是你自己给自己划定界限不往前走呀。”

13. 子谓子夏曰：“女为君子儒，无为小人儒。”

孔子对子夏说：“你要做君子式的儒者，不要做小人般的儒者。”

14. 子游为武城[③]宰。子曰：“女得人焉尔[④]乎？”曰：“有澹台灭明[⑤]者，行不由径[⑥]，非公事，未尝至于偃[⑦]之室也。”

子游做了武城的长官。孔子问他：“你在那里找到人才了吗？”子游回答说：“有一个叫澹台灭明的人，从来不走邪路，不是公事，绝不到我居处来。”

---

① 说：音 yuè，同悦。
② 画：划定界限，停止前进。
③ 武城：鲁国的小城邑，在今山东费县境内。
④ 焉尔乎：此三个字都是语助词。
⑤ 澹台灭明：姓澹台名灭明，字子羽，武城人，孔子弟子。
⑥ 径：小路，引申为邪路。
⑦ 偃：言偃，即子游，这是他自称其名。

15. The Master said, '***Meng chih Fan***[1] was not given to boasting. When the army was ***routed***[2], he stayed in the rear. But on entering the gate, he goaded his horse on, saying, 'I did not lag behind out of ***presumption***[3]. It was simply that my horse refused to go forward.'

16. The Master said, 'You may have the good looks of Sung Chao, but you will find it difficult to escape ***unscathed***[4] in this world if you do not, at the same time, have the ***eloquence***[5] of the ***Priest T'uo***[6].'

17. The Master said, 'Who can go out without using the door? Why, then, does no one follow this Way?'

18. The Master said, 'When there is a ***preponderance***[7] of native substance over acquired refinement, the result will be ***churlishness***[8]. When there is a preponderance of acquired refinement over native substance, the result will be ***pedantry***[9]. Only a well-balanced ***admixture***[10] of these two will result in gentlemanliness.'

Notes

1 Meng chih Fan 孟之反，鲁国大夫

2 rout [raut] *v.* 使溃退，打败

3 presumption [priˈzʌmpʃən] *n.* 自以为是，放肆

4 unscathed [ʌnˈskeiðd] *a.* 未受伤的

5 eloquence [ˈeləkwəns] *n.* 雄辩，口才

6 Priest T'uo 祝鮀，卫国大夫

7 preponderance [priˈpɔndərəns] *n.* 优势

8 churlishness [ˈtʃə:liʃnis] *n.* 粗暴，粗野

9 pedantry [ˈpedəntri] *n.* 迂腐；卖弄学问

10 admixture [ædˈmikstʃə] *n.* 混合

15. 子曰："孟之反①不伐②，奔③而殿④，将入门，策其马，曰：'非敢后也，马不进也。'"

孔子说："孟之反这个人从来不自夸。（当在抵御齐国的战役中）军队溃退时，他走在最后，掩护全军；快要进城门的时候，他便鞭打着自己的马说，'不是我勇于殿后，而是马跑得不快的缘故。'"

16. 子曰："不有祝鮀⑤之佞，而⑥有宋朝⑦之美，难乎免于今之世矣。"

孔子说："没有祝鮀那样的口才，也没有宋朝那样的美貌，那在今天的社会上处世立足就比较困难了。"

17. 子曰："谁能出不由户，何莫由斯道也？"

孔子说："有谁能不经过屋门而走出去呢？为什么没有人走（我所指出的）这条道路呢？"

18. 子曰："质胜文则野，文胜质则史⑧。文质彬彬⑨，然后君子。"

---

① 孟之反：名侧，鲁国大夫。
② 伐：夸耀。
③ 奔：败走。
④ 殿：殿后，在全军最后作掩护。
⑤ 祝鮀：鮀，音 tuó。字子鱼，卫国大夫，有口才，以能言善辩受到卫灵公重用。
⑥ 而：这里是"与"的意思。
⑦ 宋朝：宋国的公子朝，《左传》中曾记载他因美丽而惹乱的事情。
⑧ 史：古代起草文书的官员。
⑨ 文质彬彬：原意为文与质两种品质的适当结合，以后被用来描写文雅有礼的人。

19. The Master said, 'That a man lives is because he is straight. That a man who ***dupes***[1] others survives is because he has been fortunate enough to be spared.'

20. The Master said, 'To be fond of something is better than merely to know it, and to find joy in it is better than merely to be fond of it.'

21. The Master said, 'You can tell those who are above ***average***[2] about the best, but not those who are below average.'

22. Fan Ch'iu asked about wisdom. The Master said, 'To work for the things the common people have a right to and to keep one's distance from the gods and spirits while showing them reverence can be called wisdom.'

Fan Ch'iu asked about benevolence. The Master said, 'The benevolent man ***reaps***[3] the benefit only after overcoming difficulties. That can be called benevolence.'

Notes

1 dupe [dju:p] *v.* 欺骗

2 average [ˈævəridʒ] *n.* 中等

3 reap [ri:p] *v.* 收获

孔子说："质朴多于文采，就会流于粗俗；文采多于质朴，就流于虚伪浮夸。只有质朴和文采配合恰当，才能成为君子。"

19. 子曰："人之生也直，罔① 之生也幸而免。"

孔子说："一个人生存是靠正直，至于不正直的人也能生存，那是他侥幸地避免了灾祸。"

20. 子曰："知之者② 不如好之者，好之者不如乐之者。"

孔子说："（对任何学问和事业）懂得它的人，不如爱好它的人；爱好它的人，又不如以它为乐的人。"

21. 子曰："中人以上，可以语上也；中人以下，不可以语上也。"

孔子说："具有中等以上才智的人，可以给他讲授高深的学问；只有中等水平以下才智的人，就不能告诉他太高深的知识。"

22. 樊迟③ 问知。子曰："务民之义，敬鬼神而远之，可谓知矣。"问仁。曰："仁者先难而后获④，可谓仁矣。"

樊迟问孔子怎样才算是智，孔子说："专心教导百姓遵从义理道德，对鬼神心存敬畏但又

---

① 罔：诬罔不直的人。

② 知之者：这个和后面的三个"之"字代表什么并不明确。从孔子的思想看，可以假定它代表"道"或真理。

③ 樊迟：孔子的学生，名樊须，字子迟，故称樊迟。

④ 先难而后获：先付出力量，然后再求收获。

23. The Master said, 'The wise find joy in water; the benevolent find joy in mountains. The wise are active; the benevolent are still. The wise are joyful; the benevolent are ***long-lived***[1].'

24. The Master said, 'At one ***stroke***[2] Ch'i can be made into a Lu, and Lu, at one stroke, can be made to attain the Way.'

25. The Master said, 'A ***ku***[3] that is not truly a *ku. A ku* indeed! A *ku* indeed!'

26. Tsai Wo asked, 'If a benevolent man was told that there was another benevolent man in the well, would he, ***nevertheless***[4], go and join him?'

The Master said, 'Why should that be the case? A gentleman can be sent there, but cannot be ***lured***[5] into a ***trap***[6]. He can be ***deceived***[7], but cannot be duped.'

Notes

1 long-lived ['lɔŋ'livd] *a.* 长寿的

2 stroke [strəuk] *n.* 打，击；微小的举动

3 *ku* 觚，盛酒的器具

4 nevertheless [ˌnevəðə'les] *ad.* 然而

5 lure [luə] *v.* 引诱

6 trap [træp] *n.* 陷阱，圈套，诡计

7 deceive [di'siːv] *v.* 欺骗

要远离它，这样就算是智了。樊迟又问什么样是仁。孔子说：有仁德的人先付出力量，然后再求收获，这可以说是仁了。”

23. 子曰：“知者乐水，仁者乐山①；知者动，仁者静；知者乐，仁者寿。”

孔子说：“聪明的人爱水（因为他像水一样灵动），仁德的人爱山(因为他像山一样稳重)。聪明人活泼，仁德人沉静。聪明人快乐，仁德人长寿。”

24. 子曰：“齐一变，至于鲁；鲁一变，至于道。”

孔子说：“齐国（的政治和教育）稍微改变一下，便可以达到鲁国的程度了；鲁国（的政治和教育）再稍有变革，便能合乎大道了。”

25. 子曰：“觚② 不觚，觚哉！觚哉！”

孔子说：“觚不像觚了，这也算是觚吗？这也算是觚吗？”

26. 宰我问曰：“仁者虽告之曰井有仁③ 焉，其从之也？”子曰：“何为其然也？君子可逝④ 也，不可陷⑤ 也；可欺也，不可罔也。”

宰我问孔子：“有仁德的人，就是告诉他井

① 知者乐水，仁者乐山：“知”，音 zhì，同“智”；乐，古音 yào，喜爱的意思。

② 觚：音 gū，古代盛酒的器具，上圆下方，有棱，容量约有二升。后来觚被改变了，所以孔子认为觚不像觚。

③ 仁：这里指有仁德的人。

④ 逝：往。

⑤ 陷：陷入。

27. The Master said, 'The gentleman widely ***versed in***[1] culture but brought back to essentials by the rites can, I suppose, be ***relied upon***[2] not to turn against what he stood for.'

28. The Master went to see Nan Tzu.* Tzu-lu was displeased. The Master swore, 'If I have done anything improper, may Heaven's ***curse***[3] be on me, may Heaven's curse be on me!'

29. The Master said, '***Supreme***[4] indeed is the Mean as a moral virtue. It has been rare among the common people for quite a long time.'

30. Tzu-kung said, 'If there were a man who gave ***extensively***[5]

* The notorious wife of Duke Ling of Wei.

里掉下去一位仁人了，他会跟着下去吗？”孔子说：“为什么要这样做呢？可以叫君子远远走开不再回来，却不可以陷害他；可以欺骗他，却不可以愚弄他。”

27. 子曰：“君子博学于文[①]，约之以礼，亦可以弗畔[②] 矣夫。”

孔子说：“君子广泛地学习古代的文化典籍，再用礼仪约束自己，就可以不离经叛道了。”

28. 子见南子[③]，子路不说[④] 。夫子矢[⑤] 之曰：“予所否[⑥] 者，天厌之！天厌之！”

孔子去和南子见面，子路很不高兴。孔子发誓道：“如果我做什么不正当的事，让上天谴责我吧！让上天谴责我吧！”

29. 子曰：“中庸[⑦] 之为德也，其至矣乎！民鲜久矣。”

孔子说：“中庸作为一种道德，应该是最高的了吧！人们缺少这种道德已经很久了。”

30. 子贡[⑧]曰：“如有博施于民而能济众，何

Notes

1 versed in 在…方面有造诣，熟练的，精通的

2 rely upon 依靠，依赖

3 curse [kə:s] *n.* 诅咒，谴责

4 supreme [sju:ˈpri:m] *a.* 最高的

5 extensively [ikˈstensivli] *ad.* 广泛地

---

① 文：指各种文献、经典。

② 畔：同“叛”。

③ 南子：卫国灵公的夫人，当时实际上左右着卫国政权，有淫乱的行为。

④ 说：音 yuè，同“悦”。

⑤ 矢：同“誓”，此处讲发誓。

⑥ 否：不对，不是，指做了不正当的事。

⑦ 中庸：中，谓之无过无不及。庸，平常。

⑧ 子贡：端木赐，字子贡，是孔子的重要门徒之一，他口才好，是位外交家。

to the common people and brought help to the multitude, what would you think of him? Could he be called benevolent?'

The Master said, 'It is no longer a matter of benevolence with such a man. If you must describe him, "***sage***[1]" is, perhaps, the right word. Even Yao and Shun would have found it difficult to ***accomplish***[2] as much. Now, on the other hand, a benevolent man helps others to take their stand ***in so far as***[3] he himself wishes to take his stand,[*] and gets others there in so far as he himself wishes to get there. The ability to take as ***analogy***[4] what is near ***at hand***[5†] can be called the method of benevolence.'

---

* It is on the rites that one takes one's stand. Cf. Take your stand on the rites, (VIII.8).

† viz., oneself.

如？可谓仁乎？”子曰：“何事于仁？必也圣乎！尧、舜[①]其犹病诸！夫仁者，己欲立而立人，己欲达而达人[②]。能近取譬[③]，可谓仁之方也已。”

子贡说：“假若有一个人，他能广泛地给人民以好处，又能帮助大家生活得很好，怎么样？可以算是仁人了吗？”孔子说：“这怎么会只是仁者，一定是圣德了！就连尧、舜都不一定能做到这样呢！仁是什么呢？就是自己要站得住，同时也帮助别人站得住；自己要事事行得通，同时也帮助别人事事行得通。凡事能就近以自己作比，而推及别人，可以说就是实行仁的方法了。”

Notes

1 sage [seidʒ] *n.* 圣人

2 accomplish [ə'kɔmpliʃ] *v.* 做成功，完成

3 in so far as 到…的程度，就…来说

4 analogy [ə'nælədʒi] *n.* 类比

5 at hand 在手边

① 尧、舜：古代传说中的圣君。

② 己欲达而达人：另一种解释是：自己想理解，也帮助别人理解。

③ 能近取譬：从自己的愿望出发，推己及人。

Book VII

1. The Master said, 'I ***transmit***[1] but do not ***innovate***[2]; I am truthful in what I say and ***devoted to***[3] antiquity. I ***venture***[4] to compare myself to our ***Old P'eng***[5].'*

2. The Master said, 'Quietly to store up knowledge in my mind, to learn without ***flagging***[6], to teach without growing weary, these present me with no difficulties.'

3. The Master said, 'It is these things that cause me concern: failure to ***cultivate***[7] virtue, failure to go more deeply into what I

* It is not clear who Old P'eng was.

卷　七

1. 子曰："述而不作[①]，信而好古，窃比于我老彭[②]。"

孔子说："只传述而不创作，相信并且喜好古代的东西，我私下里把自己比做老彭。"

2. 子曰："默而识[③]之，学而不厌，诲人不倦，何有于我哉[④]？"

孔子说："把所学到的知识默默地记在心里，努力学习而不厌烦，教导别人而不疲倦，这对我有什么困难呢？"

3. 子曰："德之不修，学之不讲，闻义不

Notes

1 transmit [trænz'mit] *v.* 传播，传送
2 innovate ['inəveit] *v.* 创新
3 devote to 致力于
4 venture ['ventʃə] *v.* 冒险，敢于
5 Old P'eng 老彭
6 flag [flæg] *v.* 变得疲倦，衰弱
7 cultivate ['kʌltiveit] *v.* 培养；陶冶

---

① 述而不作：这表示孔子认为他的思想是其前代圣人思想的继续和阐明。他整理古籍，但并不著书，也许与这种认识有关。

② 老彭：究竟指谁，尚无定论。有人认为指老子和彭祖（古代一个长寿的贵族），也有人认为指商代的一个名老彭的大夫。

③ 识：音 zhì，记住。此句中的"之"应代表知识。

④ 何有于我哉：另一种理解是"我做到哪些呢？"

have learned, inability, when I am told what is right, to move to where it is, and inability to reform myself when I have defects.'

4. During his leisure moments, the Master remained correct though ***relaxed***[1].

5. The Master said, 'How I have gone downhill! It has been such a long time since I dreamt of the ***Duke of Chou***[2].'

6. The Master said, 'I set my heart on the Way, base myself on virtue, lean upon benevolence for support and take my ***recreation***[3] in the arts.'

7. The Master said, 'I have never denied instruction to anyone who, of his own accord, has given me so much as a ***bundle***[4] of dried meat as a present.'

能徙[①]，不善不能改，是吾忧也。”

孔子说：“品德不培养，学问不讲习，听到义不能去做，有了缺点不能改正，这些都是我所忧虑的事情。”

4. 子之燕居[②]，申申[③] 如也；夭夭[④] 如也。

孔子闲居在家里的时候，衣冠整洁，仪态温和，悠闲自在。

5. 子曰：“甚矣吾衰也！久矣吾不复梦见周公[⑤]。”

孔子说：“我衰老得多厉害呀！我已经很长时间没再梦见周公了！”

6. 子曰：“志于道，据于德，依于仁，游于艺[⑥]。”

孔子说：“以道为志向，以德为根据，以仁为凭借，游憩于礼、乐、射、御、书、数六艺之中。”

7. 子曰：“自行束脩[⑦] 以上，吾未尝无诲焉。”

Notes

1 relaxed [ri'lækst] *a.* 松懈的；悠闲的

2 Duke of Chou 周公

3 recreation [ˌrekri'eiʃn] *n.* 娱乐

4 bundle ['bʌndl] *n.* 捆，束

---

① 徙：音 xǐ，迁移。此处指靠近义、做到义。

② 燕居：安居、家居、闲居。

③ 申申：衣冠整洁。

④ 夭夭：行动迟缓、斯文和舒和的样子。

⑤ 周公：姓姬名旦，周文王的儿子，周武王的弟弟，成王的叔父，鲁国国君的始祖，传说是西周典章制度的制定者，他是孔子所崇拜的所谓“圣人”之一。

⑥ 游于艺：“艺”指六艺，即礼、乐、射、御、书、数。人应愉快地学习六艺，如游憩其中。

⑦ 束脩：脩，音 xiū，干肉，又叫脯。束脩就是 10 条干肉。孔子要求他的学生，初次见面时要拿十余干肉作为学费。后来，就把学生奉给老师的学费叫做“束脩”。

8. The Master said, 'I never ***enlighten***[1] anyone who has not been driven to ***distraction***[2] by trying to understand a difficulty or who has not got into a ***frenzy***[3] trying to put his ideas into words.

'When I have pointed out one corner of a square to anyone and he does not come back with the other three, I will not point it out to him a second time.'

9. When eating in the presence of one who had been ***bereaved***[4], the Master never ate his fill.

10. On a day he had wept, the Master did not sing.

11. The Master said to Yen Yüan, 'Only you and I have the ability to go forward when employed and to stay out of sight when ***set aside***[5].'

Tzu-lu said, 'If you were leading the ***Three Armies***[6] whom would you take with you?'

The Master said, 'I would not take with me anyone who would try to fight a tiger with his bare hands or to walk across the River* and die in the process without ***regrets***[7]. If I took anyone it would have to be a man who, when faced with a task, was fearful of failure and who, while fond of making plans, was capable of successful ***execution***[8].'

---

* In ancient Chinese literature, 'the River' meant the Yellow River.

Notes

1 enlighten [in'laitən] *v.* 启发

2 distraction [di'strækʃən] *n.* 分心；困惑

3 frenzy ['frenzi] *n.* 疯狂，狂乱

4 bereave [bi'ri:v] *v.* 使丧失

5 set aside 不理会

6 Three Armies 三军，当时大国所有的军队

7 regret [ri'gret] *n.* 遗憾，后悔

8 execution [ˌeksi'kju:ʃən] *n.* 实行；完成

孔子说："只要自愿拿学礼来见我的人，我从来没有不教导的。"

8. 子曰："不愤① 不启，不悱② 不发。举一隅不以三隅反，则不复也。"

孔子说："教导学生，不到他想求明白而不得的时候，不去开导他；不到他想说却说不出来的时候，不去启发他。教给他事物的一个方面，他却不能由此而推知其他几个方面的东西，那就不用再教他了。"

9. 子食于有丧者之侧，未尝饱也。

孔子在服丧的人旁边吃饭，从来没有吃饱过。

10. 子于是日哭，则不歌。

孔子如在一天曾哭泣，就不再唱歌了。

11. 子谓颜渊曰："用之则行，舍之则藏③，惟我与尔有是夫④！"子路曰："子行三军⑤，则谁与⑥？"子曰："暴虎⑦冯河⑧，死而无悔者，吾不与也。必也临事而惧⑨，好谋而成者也。"

孔子对颜渊说："如果任用我，我就去干；

---

① 愤：心求通而尚未通。

② 悱：音 fěi，口欲言而不能言。

③ 舍之则藏：舍，舍弃，不用。藏，隐藏。

④ 夫：语气词，相当于"吧"。

⑤ 三军：是当时大国所有的军队，每军约 12,500 人。

⑥ 与：在一起的意思。

⑦ 暴虎：空拳赤手与老虎进行搏斗。

⑧ 冯河：无船而徒步过河；冯，音 píng。

⑨ 临事不惧：惧是谨慎、警惕的意思。遇到事情便格外小心谨慎。

12. The Master said, 'If wealth were a ***permissible***[1] ***pursuit***[2], I would be willing even to act as a guard holding a whip outside the market place. If it is not, I shall follow my own preferences.'

13. ***Fasting***[3], war and sickness were the things over which the Master exercised care.

14. The Master heard the ***shao***[4*] in ***Ch'i***[5] and for three months did not notice the taste of the meat he ate. He said, 'I never dreamt that the joys of music could reach such ***heights***[6].'

---

* The music of Shun. Cf. III.25.

Notes

1 permissible [pə'misəbl] *a.* 可允许的

2 pursuit [pə'sju:t] *n.* 追求，寻求

3 fasting ['fɑ:stiŋ] *n.* 斋戒

4 *shao*《韶》

5 Ch'i 齐国

6 height [hait] *n.* 高度；极致

不用我，我就隐藏起来，只有我和你才能做到这样吧！”

子路问孔子说：“老师您如果统帅三军，那么将与谁在一起共事呢？”孔子说：“赤手空拳和老虎搏斗，徒步涉水过河，死了都不会后悔的人，我是不会和他在一起共事的。我要找的，一定是遇事小心谨慎、善于谋划，最终能完成任务的人。”

12. 子曰：“富①而可求②也；虽执鞭之士③，吾亦为之。如不可求，从吾所好。”

孔子说：“如果富贵合乎于道就可以去追求，即使是做地位低下的下等差事，我也愿意。如果得到富贵的方法不合于道，那就还是按我的爱好去干事吧。”

13. 子之所慎：齐④、战、疾。

孔子所小心慎重对待的事有三件：斋戒，战争，疾病。

14. 子在齐闻《韶》⑤，三月不知肉味，曰：“不图为乐之至于斯也。”

孔子在齐国听到《韶》乐后，有很长时间

---

① 富：指升官发财。

② 求：指合于道，可以去求。

③ 执鞭之士：古代为天子、诸侯和官员出入时手执皮鞭开路的人。意思指地位低下的职事。另一种说法是市场的守门人，手执皮鞭来维持秩序。

④ 齐：同斋，斋戒。古人在祭祀前要沐浴更衣，不吃荤，不饮酒，不与妻妾同寝，整洁身心，表示虔诚之心，这叫做斋戒。

⑤ 《韶》：舜时古乐曲名。

15. ***Jan Yu***[1] said, 'Is the Master on the side of the Lord of Wei?' *

Tzu-kung said, 'Well, I shall put the question to him.'

He went in and said, 'What sort of men were Po Yi and Shu Ch'i?'

'They were ***excellent***[2] men of old.'

'Did they have any ***complaints***[3]?'

'They sought benevolence and got it. So why should they have any complaints?'

When Tzu-kung came out, he said, 'The Master is not on his side.'

16. The Master said, 'In the eating of ***coarse***[4] rice and the drinking of water, the using of one's elbow for a ***pillow***[5], joy is to be found. Wealth and rank ***attained***[6] through immoral means have as much to do with me as passing clouds.'

---

* i.e., Che, known in history as the Ousted Duke, son of Prince K'uai K'ui who was son of Duke Ling. After failing in an attempt to kill Nan Tzu, the notorious wife of his father, Prince K'uai K'ui fled to Chin. On the death of Duke Ling, Che came to the throne. With the backing of the Chin army, Prince K'uai K'ui managed to install himself in the city of Ch'i in Wei, waiting for an opportunity to oust his son. At that time Confucius was inWei, and what Jan Yu wanted to know was whether he was for Che.

Notes

1 Jan Yu 冉有

2 excellent ['eksələnt] *a.* 杰出的

3 complaint [kəm'pleint] *n.* 抱怨

4 coarse [kɔːs] *a.* 粗糙的；质差的

5 pillow ['piləu] *n.* 枕头

6 attain [ə'tein] *v.* 达到，获取

吃饭时也尝不出肉的滋味，他说，"想不到《韶》乐的美达到了这样迷人的程度。"

15. 冉有曰："夫子为① 卫君② 乎？"子贡曰："诺③，吾将问之。"入，曰："伯夷、叔齐何人也？"曰："古之贤人也。"曰："怨乎？"曰："求仁而得仁，又何怨。"出，曰："夫子不为也。"

冉有（问子贡）说："老师会帮助卫国的国君吗？"子贡说："嗯，我去问问他。"

于是子贡进去拜见老师，问道："伯夷、叔齐是什么样的人呢？"孔子说："古代的贤人。"子贡问："他们（互相推让，都不肯做孤竹国的国君，结果都跑到国外）有怨恨吗？"孔子说："他们求仁而得到了仁，为什么有怨恨呢？"子贡出来对冉有说：老师不会帮助卫君。"

16. 子曰："饭疏食④ 饮水，曲肱⑤ 而枕之，乐亦在其中矣。不义而富且贵，于我如浮云。"

孔子说："吃粗粮，喝白水，弯起胳膊当枕头，乐趣也就在这里面了。用不正当的手段得来的富与贵，对我来说就像是天空一吹即散的云彩一样。"

---

① 为：这里是帮助的意思。

② 卫君：卫出公辄，是卫灵公的孙子。公元前 492 年～公元前 481 年在位。他的父亲因谋杀南子而被卫灵公驱逐出国。灵公死后，辄被立为国君，其父回国与他争位。

③ 诺：答应的说法。

④ 饭疏食，饭，这里是"吃"的意思，作动词。疏食即粗粮。

⑤ 曲肱：肱，音 gōng，胳膊，由肩至肘的部位。曲肱，即弯着胳膊。

17. The Master said, 'Grant me a few more years so that I may study at the age of fifty and I shall be free from major errors.'

18. What the Master used the correct ***pronunciation***[1] for: the *Odes*, the *Book of History* and the performance of the rites. In all these ***cases***[2] he used the correct pronunciation.

19. ***The Governor of She***[3] asked Tzu-lu about Confucius. Tzu-lu did not answer. The Master said, 'Why did you not simply say something to this effect: he is the sort of man who forgets to eat when he tries to solve a problem that has been driving him to distraction, who is so full of joy that he forgets his worries and who does not notice the ***onset***[4] of old age?'

20. The Master said, 'I was not born with knowledge but, being fond of antiquity, I am quick to seek it.'

Notes

1 pronunciation [prəˌnʌnsiˈeiʃən] *n.* 发音

2 case [keis] *n.* 情况，情形

3 the Governor of She 叶公，原名沈诸梁

4 onset [ˈɔnset] *n.* 开始

17. 子曰：“加① 我数年，五十以学易②，可以无大过矣。”

孔子说：“假如再多给我几年时间，到 50 岁时候去学习《易经》，就可以没有什么大过错了。”

18. 子所雅言③，《诗》、《书》、执礼，皆雅言也。

孔子有用普通话的时候，如他读《诗》、《书》，赞礼，都用普通话。

19. 叶公④ 问孔子于子路⑤，子路不对。子曰：“女奚不曰，其为人也，发愤忘食，乐以忘忧，不知老之将至云尔⑥ 。”

叶公问子路孔子是什么样的人，子路没回答。后来孔子对子路说：“你为什么不这样说：他的为人，用功便忘记吃饭，快乐便忘记忧愁，不晓得衰老会要到来，如此而已。”

20. 子曰：“我非生而知之者，好古，敏以求之⑦ 者也。”

① 加：这里通“假”字，给予的意思。

② 易：指《周易》，古代占卜用的一部书。

③ 雅言：周王朝的京畿之地在今陕西地区，以陕西语音为标准音的周王朝官话，在当时被称做“雅言”。孔子平日谈话时用鲁国的方言，但在诵读《诗》、《书》和赞礼时，则以当时陕西语音为准。

④ 叶公：楚国叶县的县长，名叫沈诸梁，是位贤官。

⑤ 子路：孔子门徒。

⑥ 云尔：如此而已。

⑦ 知之，求之：这两个“之”字代表什么并不明确，语译中姑且用“知识”作为两个动词的宾语。也可以认为“之”字代表“道”。

21. The topics the Master did not speak of were ***prodigies***[1], ***force***[2], ***disorder***[3] and gods.

22. The Master said, 'Even when walking in the company of two other men, I am bound to be able to learn from them. The good points of the one I copy; the bad points of the other I correct in myself.'

23. The Master said, 'Heaven is ***author***[4] of the ***virtue***[5] that is in me. What can ***Huan T'ui***[6] do to me?*

24. The Master said, 'My friends, do you think I am ***secretive***[7]? There is nothing which I hide from you. There is nothing I do which I do not share with you, my friends. There is Ch'iu for you.'

25. The Master instructs under four heads: culture, moral ***conduct***[8], doing one's best and being ***trustworthy***[9] in what one says.

---

* According to tradition, this was said on the occasion when Huan T'ui, the Minister of War in Sung, attempted to kill him.

孔子说："我不是生来就有知识的人，只是爱好古代文化，勤奋敏捷去求索知识的人。"

21. 子不语怪、力、乱、神。

孔子不谈论关于怪异、强力、叛乱和鬼神的事。

22. 子曰："三人行，必有我师焉。择其善者而从之，其不善者而改之。"

孔子说："几个人在一起做事，其中一定有可以为我所取法的人：我选择他善的品德向他学习，看到他不善的地方就作为借鉴，改掉自己的缺点。"

23. 子曰："天生德于予，桓魋①其如予何？"

孔子说："上天把高尚的品德赋予了我，桓魋又能把我怎么样呢？"

24. 子曰："二三子②以我为隐乎？吾无隐乎尔。吾无行而不与二三子者，是丘也。"

孔子说："学生们，你们以为我（在教导你们方面）对你们有什么隐瞒的吗？我丝毫没有隐瞒。我没有什么知识是不教授给你们的。我孔丘就是这样的人。"

25. 子以四教：文③、行④、忠⑤、信⑥。

Notes

1 prodigy ['prɔdidʒi] *n.* 奇事

2 force [fɔ:s] *n.* 力量

3 disorder [dis'ɔ:də] *n.* 混乱，动乱

4 author ['ɔ:θə] *n.* 创始人

5 virtue ['və:tju] *n.* 美德

6 Huan T'ui 桓魋，在宋国主管军事行政

7 secretive['si:kritiv] *a.* 隐藏的

8 conduct [kən'dʌkt] *n.* 行为，品行

9 trustworthy ['trʌstwə:ði] *a.* 可信的，可靠的

---

① 桓魋：魋，音 tuí，任宋国主管军事行政的官——司马，是宋桓公的后代。

② 二三子：这里指孔子的学生们。

③ 文：文献、古籍等。

④ 行：指德行，也指社会实践方面的内容。

⑤ 忠：尽己之谓忠，对人尽心竭力的意思。

⑥ 信：以实之谓信。诚实的意思。

26. The Master said, 'I have no hopes of meeting a sage. I would be content if I met someone who is a gentleman.'

The Master said, 'I have no hopes of meeting a good man. I would be ***content***[1] if I met someone who has ***constancy***[2]. It is hard for a man to have constancy who claims to have when he is wanting, to be full when he is empty and to be comfortable when he is in straitened circumstances.'

27. The Master used a fishing line but not a ***cable***[3*]; he used a ***corded***[4] ***arrow***[5] but not to shoot at roosting birds.

28. The Master said, 'There are ***presumably***[6] men who innovate without possessing knowledge, but that is not a fault I have. I use my ears widely and follow what is good in what I have heard; I use my eyes widely and retain what I have seen in my mind. This ***constitutes***[7] a lower level of knowledge.'

---

* Attached to a net.

孔子教授学生四项内容：历代文献、社会生活的实践、对待别人的忠诚、与人交际的信实。

26. 子曰："圣人吾不得而见之矣！得见君子者，斯① 可矣。"子曰："善人吾不得而见之矣！得见有恒② 者，斯可矣。亡而为有，虚而为盈，约③ 而为泰④ ，难乎有恒矣。"

孔子说："圣人我是不可能看到了，能看到君子也就可以了。"孔子又说："善人我不可能看到了，能见到有一定操守的人也就可以了。本来没有，却装做有；本来空虚，却装做充足；本来穷困，却装做富足，这样的人便难以保持一定操守了。"

27. 子钓而不纲⑤，弋⑥ 不射宿⑦ 。

孔子只用有一个渔钩的钓竿钓鱼，而不用有许多渔钩的大绳钓鱼；只射飞鸟，而不射归巢歇宿的鸟。

28. 子曰："盖有不知而作之者，我无是也。多闻，择其善者而从之，多见而识之，知之次也。"

---

① 斯：就。
② 恒：指恒心。
③ 约：穷困。
④ 泰：这里是奢侈的意思。
⑤ 纲：大绳。这里作动词用。在水面上拉一根大绳，在大绳上系许多渔钩来钓鱼，叫纲。
⑥ 弋：音 yì，用带绳子的箭来射鸟。
⑦ 宿：指归巢歇宿的鸟儿。

Notes

1 content ['kɔntent] *a.* 满足的，满意的

2 constancy ['kɔnstənsi] *n.* 恒久不变，坚定不移

3 cable ['keibl] *n.* 索，缆

4 corded ['kɔ:did] *a.* 绳制的，用绳捆扎的

5 arrow ['ærəu] *n.* 箭

6 presumably [pri'zju:məbli] *ad.* 大概，可能

7 constitute ['kɔnstitju:t] *v.* 组成

29. People of ***Hu Hsiang***[1] were difficult to talk to. A boy was received and the disciples were ***perplexed***[2]. The Master said, 'Approval of his coming does not mean approval of him when he is not here. Why should we be so ***exacting***[3]? When a man comes after having ***purified***[4] himself, we approve of his purification but we cannot ***vouch for***[5] his past.'*

30. The Master said, 'Is benevolence really far away? ***No sooner*** do I desire it ***than***[6] it is here.'

31. Ch'en Ssu-pai asked whether ***Duke Chao***[7] was versed in the rites. Confucius said, 'Yes.'

---

* It has been suggested that this sentence should stand at the beginning of Confucius' remark.

Notes

1 Hu Hsiang
互乡，地名

2 perplexed [pə'plekst] *a.* 迷惑的

3 exacting [ig'zæktiŋ] *a.* 严格的，严厉的

4 purify ['pjuərifai] *v.* 净化，使纯净

5 vouch for 担保

6 no sooner… than 一…就…

7 Duke Chao
昭公，鲁国的君主

孔子说："大概有一种人，他什么都不懂却在那里凭空创造，但我没有这样做过。广泛听取见解，选择其中好的来学习；多观察事物，然后记在心里，这是次一等的智慧。"

29. 互乡① 难与言，童子见，门人惑。子曰："与② 其进③ 也，不与其退也，唯何甚？人洁己④ 以进，与其洁也，不保其往⑤ 也。"

（孔子认为）很难与互乡那个地方的人交流，但互乡的一个年轻人却受到了孔子的接见，学生们为此都感到迷惑不解。孔子说："我们肯定他的进步，不肯定他的倒退。何必做得太过分呢？别人改正了错误以求进步，我们要肯定他改正了错误，不要总抓住他的过去不罢休。"

30. 子曰："仁远乎哉？我欲仁，斯仁至矣。"

孔子说："仁德离我们很远吗？只要我们想达到仁德，仁德就会来了。"

31. 陈司败⑥ 问："昭公⑦ 知礼乎？"孔子曰：

① 互乡：地名，具体所在已无可考。
② 与：赞许。
③ 进、退：一说进步、退步；一说进见请教，退出以后的作为。
④ 洁己：洁身自好，努力修养，成为有德之人。
⑤ 不保其往：保，一说担保，一说保守。往，一说过去，一说将来。
⑥ 陈司败：陈国主管司法的官，姓名不详，也有人说是齐国大夫，姓陈名司败。
⑦ 昭公：鲁国的君主，名惆，音 chóu，公元前 541—公元前 510 年在位。"昭" 是谥号。

After Confucius had gone, Ch'en Ssu-pai, bowing to ***Wu-ma Ch'i***[1], invited him forward and said, 'I have heard that the gentleman does not show ***partiality***[2]. Does he show it nevertheless? The Lord took as wife a daughter of Wu, who thus is of the same clan as himself,* but he allows her to be called Wu Meng Tzu.† If the Lord is versed in the rites, who isn't?'

When Wu-ma Ch'i ***recounted***[3] this to him, the Master said, 'I am a fortunate man. Whenever I make a mistake, other people are sure to notice it.'‡

32. When the Master was singing ***in the company of***[4] others and liked someone else's song, he always asked to hear it again before joining in.

33. The Master said, 'In ***unstinted***[5] effort I can compare with others, but in being a practising gentleman I have had, as yet, no success.'

---

* Bearing the name Chi.

† when she should be called Wu Chi. Calling her Wu Meng Tzu was an attempt to gloss over the fact that she shared the same clan name of Chi.

‡ Being a native of Lu, Confucius would rather be criticized for partiality than appear to be openly critical of the Duke.

Notes

1 Wu-ma Ch'i 巫马期，孔子的学生

2 partiality [ˌpɑːʃiˈæliti] *n.* 偏爱

3 recount [riˈkaunt] *v.* 讲述

4 in the company of 在…的陪同下

5 unstinted [ʌnˈstintid] *a.* 不吝惜的，足够的

"知礼。"孔子退，揖[①]巫马期[②]而进之曰："吾闻君子不党[③]，君子亦党乎？君取[④]于吴，为同姓[⑤]，谓之吴孟子[⑥]。君而知礼，孰不知礼？"巫马期以告。子曰："丘也幸，苟有过，人必知之。"

陈司败向孔子询问鲁昭公懂不懂礼，孔子说："懂礼。"孔子出去以后，陈司败便向巫马期行礼，请他走近自己，对他说："我听说君子无所偏袒，难道孔子也还包庇别人吗？鲁君从吴国娶了位夫人，吴和鲁是同姓国家，（因不便叫她做吴姬）于是称她为吴孟子。如果鲁君算是知礼，还有谁不知礼呢？"巫马期将这些话转告给孔子。孔子说："我真幸运，一旦有错，别人一定会给我指出来。"

32. 子与人歌而善，必使反之，而后和之。

孔子与别人一起唱歌，如果（那个人）唱得好，（孔子）一定请他再唱一遍，然后一起唱和他。

33. 子曰："文，莫[⑦]吾犹人也。躬行君子，

---

① 揖：做揖，行拱手礼。

② 巫马期：姓巫马名施，字子期，孔子的学生，比孔子小30岁。

③ 党：偏袒、包庇的意思。

④ 取：同娶。

⑤ 为同姓：鲁国和吴国的国君同姓姬。周礼规定：同姓不婚，昭公娶同姓女，是违礼的行为。

⑥ 吴孟子：鲁昭公夫人。春秋时代，国君夫人的称号，一般是她出生的国名加上她的姓，但因她姓姬，故称为吴孟子，而不称吴姬。

⑦ 莫：约摸、大概、差不多。

34. The Master said, 'How dare I claim to be a sage or a benevolent man? Perhaps it might be said of me that I learn without flagging and teach without growing ***weary***[1].' ***Kung-hsi Hua***[2] said, This is ***precisely***[3] where we disciples are unable to learn from your example.'

35. The Master was seriously ill. Tzu-lu asked ***permission***[4] to offer a prayer. The Master said, 'Was such a thing ever done?' Tzu-lu said, 'Yes, it was. The prayer offered was as follows: pray thus to the gods above and below.' The Master said, 'In that case, I have long been offering my prayers.'

Notes

1 weary ['wiəri] *a.* 厌倦的，疲倦的

2 Kung-hsi Hua 公西华，孔子的学生

3 precisely [pri'saisli] *ad.* 精确地，准确地

4 permission [pə'miʃən] *n.* 允许

则吾未之有得。”

孔子说：“就书本上的学问来说，大概我和别人知道的差不多。但要做一个身体力行的君子，我还没有做到。”

34. 子曰：“若圣与仁，则吾岂敢？抑① 为之② 不厌，诲人不倦，则可谓云尔③ 已矣。”公西华曰：“正唯弟子不能学也。”

孔子说：“讲到圣和仁，我怎么敢当？我不过是向圣与仁的方向不断努力去做而不感厌烦，教导别人也从不感觉疲倦，只不过如此罢了。”公西华说：“这正是我们学不会的呀。”

35. 子疾病④，子路请祷⑤。子曰：“有诸⑥？”子路对曰：“有之。《诔》⑦ 曰：‘祷尔于上下神祇⑧。’”子曰：“丘之祷久矣。”

孔子病情严重，子路向鬼神祈祷。孔子问：“有这回事吗？”子路回答道：“有的。《诔》文上说过：‘替你向天地神灵祈祷。’”孔子说：“我早就祈祷过了。”

---

① 抑：转折的语气词，“只不过是”的意思。
② 为之：指圣与仁。
③ 云尔：这样说。
④ 疾病：疾指有病，病指病情严重。
⑤ 请祷：向鬼神请求和祷告，即祈祷。
⑥ 有诸：诸，“之于”的合音。意为：有这样的事吗。
⑦ 《诔》：音 lěi，祈祷文。
⑧ 神祇：祇：音 qí，古代称天神为神，地神为祇。

36. The Master said, 'Extravagance means ***ostentation***[1], frugality means ***shabbiness***[2]. I would rather be shabby than ostentatious.'

37. The Master said, 'The gentleman is easy of mind, while the small man is always full of anxiety.'

38. The Master is cordial yet ***stern***[3], ***awe-inspiring***[4] yet not fierce, and respectful yet at ease.

Notes

1 ostentation [ˌɔstenˈteiʃən] *n.* 虚饰，卖弄

2 shabbiness [ˈʃæbinis] *n.* 破旧；寒酸

3 stern [stəːn] *a.* 严肃的

4 awe-inspiring *a.* 令人敬畏的

36. 子曰：“奢则不孙[①]，俭则固[②]。与其不孙也，宁固。”

孔子说：“奢侈了就会越礼，节俭了就会寒酸。与其越礼，宁可寒酸。”

37. 子曰：“君子坦荡荡[③]，小人长戚戚[④]。”

孔子说：“君子心胸宽广，小人总是忧愁。”

38. 子温而厉，威而不猛，恭而安。

孔子温和而又严肃，有威仪而不凶狠，庄重而又安详。

---

① 孙：同逊，恭顺。不孙，即为不顺，这里的意思是“越礼”。

② 固：简陋、鄙陋。这里是寒酸的意思。

③ 坦荡荡：心胸宽广、开阔、容忍。

④ 长戚戚：经常忧愁、烦恼的样子。

Book VIII

1. The Master said, 'Surely ***T'ai Po***[1] can be said to be of the highest virtue. Three times he ***abdicated***[2] his right to rule over the Empire, and yet he left behind nothing the common people could ***acclaim***[3].'

2. The Master said, 'Unless a man has the spirit of the rites, in being respectful he will wear himself out, in being careful he will become ***timid***[4], in having courage he will become ***unruly***[5], and in being forthright he will become ***intolerant***[6].

'When the gentleman feels ***profound***[7] affection for his parents, the common people will be ***stirred***[8] to benevolence. When he does not forget friends of long standing, the common people will not shirk their ***obligations***[9] to other people.'

卷 八

1. 子曰："泰伯[①]，其可谓至德也已矣。三[②]以天下让，民无得而称焉[③]。"

孔子说："泰伯可以说是品德最高尚的人了，多次把王位让给季历，老百姓都找不到恰当的词语来称赞他。"

2. 子曰："恭而无礼则劳，慎而无礼则葸[④]，勇而无礼则乱，直而无礼则绞[⑤]。君子笃于亲，则民兴于仁；故旧不遗，则民不偷[⑥]。"

孔子说："只是注重态度的恭敬而不以礼来指导，就未免劳倦；只知言行的谨慎却不知礼，就流于畏缩懦弱；有敢作敢为的胆量，却不用礼来制约，就会冲动招祸；太心直口快而不知

① 泰伯：周代始祖古公亶父的长子。
② 三：多次的意思。
③ 民无得而称焉：百姓找不到合适的词句来赞扬他。
④ 葸：音 xǐ，畏惧不前。
⑤ 绞：急切。
⑥ 偷：无情义。

Notes

1 T'ai Po 泰伯，周代始祖的长子

2 abdicate [ˈæbdikeit] *v.* 放弃；退位

3 acclaim [əˈkleim] *v.* 称赞

4 timid [ˈtimid] *a.* 胆小的

5 unruly [ʌnˈru:li] *a.* 难驾驭的，不守规矩的

6 intolerant [inˈtɔlərənt] *a.* 不宽容的，偏执的

7 profound [prəˈfaund] *a.* 深刻的，深切的

8 stir [stə:] *v.* 唤醒；激起

9 obligation [ˌɔbliˈgeiʃən] *n.* 义务，责任

3. When he was seriously ill Tseng Tzu ***summoned***[1] his disciples and said, 'Take a look at my hands. Take a look at my feet. The *Odes* say,

In fear and trembling,
As if approaching a deep abyss,
As if walking on thin ice.[*]

Only now am I sure of being ***spared***[2],[†] my young friends.'

4. Tseng Tzu was seriously ill. When Meng Ching Tzu visited him, this was what Tseng Tzu said,

'Sad is the cry of a dying bird;
Good are the words of a dying man.

There are three things which the gentleman values most in the Way: to stay clear of violence by putting on a serious ***countenance***[3], to come close to being trusted by setting a proper expression on his face, and to avoid being ***boorish***[4] and ***unreasonable***[5] by speaking in proper ***tones***[6]. As for the business of ***sacrificial***[7] vessels, there are

---

* Ode 195.

† i.e., to have avoided, now that he was on the point of death, the risk of the mutilation of his body — a duty which he owed to his parents.

Notes

1 summon [ˈsʌmən] *v.* 召集

2 spare [spɛə] *v.* 使免遭，不伤害

3 countenance [ˈkauntənəns] *n.* 面容

4 boorish [ˈbuəriʃ] *a.* 粗鲁的

5 unreasonable [ʌnˈri:zənəbl] *a.* 不合理的

6 tone [təun] *n.* 声调，语气

7 sacrificial [ˌsækriˈfiʃəl] *a.* 献祭的

礼，就会尖刻刺人。在上位的人如果厚待自己的亲属，老百姓当中就会兴起仁德的风气；在上位的人如果不遗弃老同事、老朋友，那老百姓就不会对人冷淡无情了。”

3. 曾子有疾，召门弟子曰：“启[①]予足！启予手！《诗》云[②]：‘战战兢兢，如临深渊，如履薄冰。’而今而后，吾知免[③]夫，小子[④]！”

曾参病得很重，他把学生召集到身边来说道：“看看我的脚！看看我的手！《诗经》上说：‘小心谨慎呀！好像站在深渊旁边，好像踩在薄冰上面。’从今以后，我知道自己的身体已经不会再受到损伤了！学生们！”

4. 曾子有疾，孟敬子[⑤]问[⑥]之。曾子言曰：“鸟之将死，其鸣也哀；人之将死，其言也善。君子所贵乎道者三：动容貌[⑦]，斯远暴慢[⑧]矣；正颜色[⑨]，斯近信矣；出辞气[⑩]，斯远鄙倍[⑪]矣。笾豆

① 启：开启，曾子让学生掀开被子看自己的手脚。
② 诗云：以下三句引自《诗经·小雅·小旻》篇。
③ 免：指身体免于损伤。
④ 小子：对弟子的称呼。
⑤ 孟敬子：即鲁国大夫孟孙捷。
⑥ 问：探望、探视。
⑦ 动容貌：使自己的仪态威严。
⑧ 暴慢：粗暴、放肆。
⑨ 正颜色：使自己的脸色庄重。
⑩ 出辞气：出言，说话。指注意说话的言辞和口气。
⑪ 鄙倍：鄙，粗野。倍同背，背理。

officials responsible for that.'

5. Tseng Tzu said, 'To be able yet to ask the advice of those who are not able. To have many talents yet to ask the advice of those who have few. To have yet to appear to want. To be full yet to appear empty.* To be ***transgressed***[1] against yet not to mind. It was towards this end that my friend† used to direct his efforts.'

6. Tseng Tzu said, 'If a man can be ***entrusted***[2] with an ***orphan***[3] six *ch'ih*‡ tall, and the fate of a state one hundred *li* square, without his being ***deflected***[4] from his purpose even in moments of crisis, is

---

* 'This is in contrast to the man cwho claims to have when he is wanting, to be full when he is empty' (VII.26).

† According to tradition, this refers to Yen Hui.

‡ The *ch'ih* in Tseng Tzu's time was much shorter than the modern foot.

之事①，则有司②存。"

曾子有病，孟敬子去探望他。曾子对他说："鸟快死了，它的叫声是悲哀的；人快死了，他说的话是善意的。君子待人接物时有三方面事项应该注重：使自己的仪态威严，这样可以避免粗暴、放肆；使自己的脸色庄重，这样就接近于诚信；使自己说话的言辞和语气谨慎小心，这样就可以避免鄙陋粗俗和错误。至于礼仪的细节，自有主管这些事务的官吏来负责。"

5. 曾子曰："以能问于不能，以多问于寡，有若无，实若虚；犯而不校③——昔者吾友④尝从事于斯矣。"

曾子说："自己有才能却向没有才能的人请教，自己知识渊博却向知识少的人请教，有学问却像没学问一样，知识很充实却好像很空虚；纵被人欺侮，也从不计较——从前我的朋友就是这样做的。"

6. 曾子说："可以托六尺之孤⑤，可以寄百

Notes

1 transgress [træns'gres] *v.* 侵犯

2 entrust [in'trʌst] *v.* 委托，托付

3 orphan ['ɔ:fən] *n.* 孤儿

4 deflect [di'flekt] *v.* 使偏离，转移

---

① 笾豆之事：笾（音 biān）和豆都是古代祭祀和典礼中的用具。

② 有司：指主管某一方面事务的官吏，这里指主管祭祀、礼仪事务的官吏。

③ 校：音 jiào，同较，计较。

④ 吾友：我的朋友。旧注上一般都认为这里指颜渊。

⑤ 托六尺之孤：孤：死去父亲的小孩叫孤，六尺指 15 岁以下，古人以七尺指成年。托孤，受君主临终前的嘱托辅佐幼君。

he not a gentleman? He is, indeed, a gentleman.'

7. Tseng Tzu said, 'A Gentleman must be strong and resolute, for his ***burden***[1] is heavy and the road is long. He takes benevolence as his burden. Is that not heavy? Only with death does the road come to an end. Is that not long?'

8. The Master said, 'Be ***stimulated***[2] by the *Odes*, take your stand on the rites and be perfected by music.'

9. The Master said, 'The common people can be made to follow a path but not to understand it.'

10. The Master said, 'Being fond of courage while ***detesting***[3] poverty will lead men to unruly behaviour. Excessive detestation of men who are not benevolent will ***provoke***[4] them to unruly behaviour.'

Notes

1 burden [ˈbəːdən] *n.* 负担

2 stimulate [ˈstimjuleit] *v.* 促进；激励

3 detest [diˈtest] *v.* 厌恶

4 provoke [prəˈvəuk] *v.* 煽动，激怒

里之命[①]，临大节而不可夺也。君子人与？君子人也。”

曾子说：“可以托付年幼的君主，可以托付国家的政权，面临生死存亡的紧急关头而不动摇屈服。这样的人是君子吗？是君子啊！”

7. 曾子曰：“士不可以不弘毅[②]，任重而道远。仁以为己任，不亦重乎？死而后已，不亦远乎？”

曾子说：“读书人不可以不刚强而有毅力，因为他责任重大，路程遥远。以实现仁德于天下为自己的责任，难道还不重大吗？奋斗终身，死而后已，难道路程还不遥远吗？”

8. 子曰：“兴[③]于《诗》，立于礼，成于乐。”

孔子说：“（人的修养）开始于学习《诗》，自立于学习《礼》，完成于学习《乐》。”

9. 子曰：“民可使由之，不可使知之。”

孔子说：“对于老百姓，可以让他们按照我们所引导的道路去走，但不可以让他们知道那是为什么。”

10. 子曰：“好勇疾[④]贫，乱也。人而不仁[⑤]，疾之已甚[⑥]，乱也。”

---

① 寄百里之命：寄，寄托、委托。百里之命，指掌握国家政权和命运。

② 弘毅：弘，广大。毅，强毅。

③ 兴：开始。

④ 疾：恨、憎恨。

⑤ 不仁：不符合仁德的人或事。

⑥ 已甚：已，太。已甚，即太过分。

11. The Master said, 'Even with a man as gifted as the Duke of Chou, if he was ***arrogant***[1] and ***miserly***[2], then the rest of his qualities would not be worthy of admiration.'

12. The Master said, 'It is not easy to find a man who can study for three years without thinking about earning a ***salary***[3].'

13. The Master said, 'Have the firm faith to devote yourself to learning, and ***abide***[4] to the death in the good way. Enter not a state that is in peril; stay not in a state that is in danger. Show yourself when the Way prevails in the Empire, but hide yourself when it does not. It is a ***shameful***[5] matter to be poor and ***humble***[6] when the Way prevails in the state. Equally, it is a shameful matter to be rich and ***noble***[7] when the Way falls into disuse in the state.'

14. The Master said, 'Do not concern yourself with matters of government unless they are the responsibility of your office.'

孔子说："喜好勇敢却又厌恶贫困，是一种祸患。太憎恨不仁德的人或事，也会出乱子。"

11. 子曰："如有周公之才之美，使骄且吝，其余不足观也已。"

孔子说："即使一个人有周公那样美好的才能，如果骄傲自大而且吝啬小气，那其他方面也就不值得一看了。"

12. 子曰："三年学，不至于谷①，不易得也。"

孔子说："读书三年并不存做官的念头，这是难得的。"

13. 子曰："笃信好学，守死善道，危邦不入，乱邦不居。天下有道则见②，无道则隐。邦有道，贫且贱焉，耻也；邦无道，富且贵焉，耻也。"

孔子说："坚定信念并努力学习，誓死捍卫并完善治国与为人的大道；不进入政局不稳的国家，不居住在动乱的国家。天下政治清明就出来工作；天下混乱就隐居。国家有道、政治清明而自己贫贱，是耻辱；国家无道、政治黑暗而自己富贵，也是耻辱。"

14. 子曰："不在其位，不谋其政。

孔子说："不在那个职位上，就不要去考虑

Notes

1 arrogant ['ærəgənt] *a.* 傲慢的

2 miserly ['maizəli] *a.* 吝啬的

3 salary ['sæləri] *n.* 薪水

4 abide [ə'baid] *v.* 遵守，履行

5 shameful ['ʃeimful] *a.* 可耻的

6 humble ['hʌmbl] *a.* 卑微的

7 noble ['nəubl] *a.* 高尚的

---

① 谷：古代以谷作为官吏的俸禄，这里用"谷"字代表做官。不至于谷，即不做官。

② 见：音 xiàn，同现。

15. The Master said, 'When Chih, the Master Musician, begins to play and when the *Kuan chü*[*] comes to its end, how the sound fills the ear!'

16. The Master said, 'Men who ***reject***[1] discipline and yet are not straight, men who are ignorant and yet not ***cautious***[2], men who are ***devoid of***[3] ability and yet not trustworthy are quite beyond my understanding.'

17. The Master said, 'Even with a man who ***urges***[4] himself on in his studies as though he was losing ground, my fear is still that he may not make it in time.'

18. The Master said, 'How ***lofty***[5] Shun and Yü were in holding ***aloof from***[6] the Empire when they were in ***possession***[7] of it.'

---

* The first ode in the Odes.

Notes

1 reject [ri'dʒekt] *v.* 拒绝，排斥

2 cautious ['kɔːʃəs] *a.* 小心的，谨慎的

3 devoid of 缺乏，没有

4 urge [əːdʒ] *v.* 催促；激励

5 lofty ['lɔfti] *a.* 崇高的

6 aloof from 远离，不参与

7 possession [pə'zeʃən] *n.* 拥有

属于那个职位才应该做的事。”

15. 子曰：“师挚之始①，《关雎》之乱②，洋洋乎盈耳哉！”

孔子说：“从太师挚演奏的音乐的序曲开始，到最后演奏《关雎》的结尾，丰富而优美的音乐就一直在我耳边回荡。”

16. 子曰：“狂③而不直，侗④ 而不愿⑤，悾悾⑥而不信，吾不知之矣。”

孔子说：“狂妄而不正直，无知而不谨慎，表面上诚恳而不信守承诺，我不知道有这样的人。”

17. 子曰：“学如不及，犹恐失之。”

孔子说：“做学问就好像（在追逐什么东西似的）生怕赶不上；（赶上了）还生怕丢掉了。”

18. 子曰：“巍巍⑦ 乎，舜禹⑧ 之有天下也而不与⑨ 焉！”

---

① 师挚之始：师挚是鲁国的太师。“始”是乐曲的开端，即序曲。古代奏乐，开端叫“升歌”，一般由太师演奏，师挚是太师，所以这里说是“师挚之始”。

② 《关雎》之乱：“始”是乐曲的开端，“乱”是乐曲的终了。“乱”是合奏乐。此时奏《关雎》乐章，所以叫“《关雎》之乱”。

③ 狂：急躁、急进。

④ 侗：音 tóng，幼稚无知。

⑤ 愿：谨慎、小心、朴实。

⑥ 悾悾：音 kōng，同空，诚恳的样子。

⑦ 巍巍：崇高、高大的样子。

⑧ 舜禹：舜是传说中的圣君明主。禹是夏朝的第一个国君。传说古时代，尧禅位给舜，舜后来又禅位给禹。

⑨ 与：参与、相关的意思。

19. The Master said, 'Great indeed was Yao as a ruler! How lofty! It is Heaven that is great and it was Yao who ***modelled***[1] himself upon it. He was so ***boundless***[2] that the common people were not able to put a name to his virtues. Lofty was he in his successes and brilliant was he in his accomplishments!'

20. Shun had five officials and the Empire was well governed. King Wu said, 'I have ten capable officials.'

Confucius commented, 'How true it is that talent is difficult to find! The period of T'ang and Yü* was rich in talent.† With a woman ***amongst***[3] them, there were, in fact, only nine,‡ The Chou continued to serve the Yin when it was in possession of two-thirds of the Empire. Its virtue can be said to have been the highest.'

---

* T'cang here is the name of Yao's dynasty and Yü the name of Shun's dynasty, not to be confused with T'ang the founder of the Yin or Shang dynasty and Yü the founder of the Hsia dynasty.

† Yet Shun had only five officials.

‡ In the case of King Wu.

Notes

1 model [ˈmɔdəl] *v.* 模仿

2 boundless [ˈbaundlis] *a.* 无限的

3 amongst [əˈmʌŋst] *prep.* 在…中间

孔子说："舜和禹多崇高伟大呀！他们虽贵为天子，富有四海，却一点也不是为了自己。"

19. 子曰："大哉尧[①] 之为君也！巍巍乎，唯天为大，唯尧则[②]之。荡荡[③] 乎，民无能名[④] 焉。巍巍乎其有成功也，焕乎其有文章！"

孔子说："尧这样的君主真伟大、真崇高啊！只有天最高最大，只有尧才能效法天的高大。他的恩德多么广博啊，百姓们不知道该用什么语言来称赞他。他的功绩多么崇高，他制定的礼仪制度多么光辉灿烂啊！"

20. 舜有臣五人[⑤] 而天下治。武王曰："予有乱臣十人[⑥]。"孔子曰："才难，不其然乎？唐虞之际[⑦]，于斯[⑧]为盛，有妇人焉[⑨]，九人而已。三分天下有其二[⑩]，以服事殷。周之德，其可谓至德也已矣。"

舜有5位贤臣，天下就被治理好了。周武

① 尧：中国古代传说中的圣君。

② 则：效法、为准。

③ 荡荡：广大的样子。

④ 名：形容、称说、称赞。

⑤ 舜有臣五人：传说是禹、稷、契、皋陶、伯益等人。契：音 xiè；陶：音 yáo。

⑥ 乱臣：据《说文》："乱，治也。"此处所说的"乱臣"，应为"治国之臣"。

⑦ 唐虞之际：传说尧在位的时代叫唐，舜在位的时代叫虞。

⑧ 斯：指周武王时期。

⑨ 有妇人焉：指武王的乱臣 10 人中有武王之妻邑姜。

⑩ 三分天下有其二：《逸周书·程典篇》说："文王令九州之侯，奉勤于商。"相传当时分 9 州，文王得 6 州，是 2/3。

21. The Master said, 'With Yü I can find no fault. He ate and drank the meanest fare while making offerings to ***ancestral***[1] spirits and gods with the utmost devotion proper to a ***descendant***[2]. He wore coarse clothes while sparing no ***splendour***[3] in his robes and caps on sacrificial occasions. He lived in lowly ***dwellings***[4] while devoting all his energy to the building of ***irrigation***[5] ***canals***[6]. With Yü I can find no fault.'

王也曾说过："我有10个帮助我治理国家的臣子。"孔子因此说："人才难得，难道不是这样吗？唐尧和虞舜时代到周武王这个时期，人才最为兴盛。但武王的10个大臣中有一人是妇女，实际上只是9个人罢了。周文王已经统治了商朝疆土的2/3，仍然殷勤侍奉商纣，周朝的道德，可以说是最高的了。"

21. 子曰："禹，吾无间① 然矣。菲② 饮食而致③ 孝乎鬼神，恶衣服而致美乎黻冕④；卑⑤ 宫室而尽力乎沟洫⑥。禹，吾无间然矣。"

孔子说："对于禹，我没有什么可以挑剔的。他自己吃的饮食很简单，却把祭品办得极丰盛；他平时穿的衣服很简朴，而祭祀时尽量穿得华美；他自己住的宫室很低矮，而把力量完全用于修治水利事宜。对于禹，我确实没有什么可以挑剔的。"

Notes

1 ancestral [æn'sestrəl] *a.* 祖先的

2 descendant [di'sendənt] *n.* 后代

3 splendour ['splendə] *n.* 华美，光彩

4 dwelling ['dweliŋ] *n.* 住所

5 irrigation [ˌiri'geiʃən] *n.* 灌溉

6 canal [kə'næl] *n.* 运河

---

① 间：空隙的意思。此处用作动词。

② 菲：菲薄，不丰厚。

③ 致：致力、努力。

④ 黻冕：音 fǔ miǎn，祭祀时穿的礼服叫黻；祭祀时戴的帽子叫冕。

⑤ 卑：低矮。

⑥ 沟洫：洫，音 xù，沟渠。

Book IX

1. The occasions on which the Master talked about profit, Destiny and benevolence were rare.

2. A man from a village in ***Ta Hsiang***[1] said, 'Great indeed is Confucius! He has wide learning but has not ***made a name for himself***[2] in any field.' The Master, on hearing of this, said, to his disciples, 'What should I make myself ***proficient***[3] in? In driving? or in archery? I think I would prefer driving.'

3. The Master said, 'A ***ceremonial***[4] cap of linen is what is prescribed by the rites. Today black silk is used instead. This is more frugal and I follow the majority. To ***prostrate***[5] oneself before

卷　九

1. 子罕[①] 言利与[②] 命与仁。

孔子很少主动谈到功利、命运和仁德。

2. 达巷党人[③] 曰："大哉孔子！博学而无所成名[④]。"子闻之，谓门弟子曰："吾何执？执御乎？执射乎？吾执御矣。"

达巷有人说："孔子真伟大啊！他学问广博，可惜没有足以树立名声的专长。"孔子听说后对他的学生说："我要专长于哪个方面呢？驾车呢？还是射箭呢？我还是驾车吧。"

3. 子曰："麻冕[⑤]，礼也；今也纯[⑥]，俭[⑦]，吾从

Notes

1 Ta Hsiang 达巷，党名，古代 500 家为一党

2 make a name for oneself 成名

3 proficient [prəˈfiʃənt] *a.* 精通的

4 ceremonial [ˌserəˈməuniəl] *a.* 礼仪的

5 prostrate [ˈprɔstreit] *v.* 使俯卧，拜倒

---

① 罕：稀少，很少。

② 与：赞同、肯定。

③ 达巷党人：古代 500 家为一党，达巷是党名。这是说达巷这地方的人。

④ 博学而无所成名：学问渊博，因而不能以某一方面来称道他。

⑤ 麻冕：麻布制成的礼帽。

⑥ 纯：丝绸，黑色的丝。

⑦ 俭：俭省，麻冕费工，用丝则俭省。

ascending[1] the steps is what is prescribed by the rites. Today one does so after having ascended them. This is casual and, though going against the majority, I follow the practice of doing so before ascending.'

4. There were four things the Master refused to have anything to do with: he refused to entertain ***conjectures***[2] or insist on certainty; he refused to be inflexible or to be ***egotistical***[3].

5. When under ***siege***[4] in K'uang, the Master said, 'With King Wen dead, is not culture *(wen)* invested here in me? If Heaven ***intends***[5] culture to be destroyed, those who come after me will not be able to have any part of it. If Heaven does not intend this culture to be destroyed, then what can the men of K'uang do to me?'

Notes

1 ascend [ə'send] *v.* 登上，爬上（梯等）

2 conjecture [kən'dʒektʃə] *v.* 猜测

3 egotistical [ˌegə'tistikəl] *a.* 自负的

4 siege [siːdʒ] *n.* 包围，围困

5 intend [in'tend] *v.* 想要，打算

众。拜下①，礼也；今拜乎上，泰② 也。虽违众，吾从下。”

孔子说：“礼帽用麻料制作，这是合于传统礼制规定的；今天大家都用黑色丝绸制作，这样比过去节省了，我赞成大家的做法。臣见国君首先要在堂下跪拜，然后升堂时又磕头，这是符合传统礼制的。今天大家都免去了堂下跪拜的礼节，只在升堂后磕头，这是倨傲的表现。虽然违反大家意愿，我仍然主张要先在堂下跪拜。”

4. 子绝四：毋意③，毋必④ ，毋固⑤，毋我⑥。

孔子杜绝了四种毛病：“不主观猜疑，不绝对肯定，不拘泥固执，不唯我独是。”

5. 子畏于匡⑦，曰：“文王⑧ 既没，文不在兹⑨ 乎？天之将丧斯文也，后死者⑩ 不得与⑪ 于斯文也；天之未丧斯文也，匡人其如予何⑫？”

---

① 拜下：大臣面见君主前，先在堂下跪拜，再到堂上跪拜。
② 泰：这里指骄纵、傲慢。
③ 意：同臆，猜想、猜疑。
④ 必：必定。
⑤ 固：固执己见。
⑥ 我：指自私，唯我独尊。
⑦ 畏于匡：匡，地名，在今河南省长垣县西南。畏，受到威胁。公元前 496 年，孔子从卫国到陈国去经过匡地。匡人曾受到鲁国阳虎的掠夺和残杀。孔子的相貌与阳虎相像，匡人误以孔子就是阳虎，所以将他围困。
⑧ 文王：周文王，姓姬名昌，西周开国之君周武王的父亲。
⑨ 兹：这里，指孔子自己。
⑩ 后死者：孔子这里指自己。
⑪ 与：同“举”，这里是掌握的意思。
⑫ 如予何：奈我何，把我怎么样。

6. The *t'ai tsai** asked Tzu-kung, 'Surely the Master is a sage, is he not? ***Otherwise***[1] why should he be skilled in so many things?' Tzu-kung said, 'It is true, Heaven set him on the path to ***sagehood***[2]. However, he is skilled in many things besides.'

The Master, on hearing of this, said, 'How well the *t'ai tsai* knows me! I was of humble station when young. That is why I am skilled in many ***menial***[3] things. Should a gentleman be skilled in many things? No, not at all.'

7. ***Lao***[4]† said, 'The Master said, "I have never been proved in office. That is why I am a ***Jack of all trades***[5]."'

8. The Master said, 'Do I possess knowledge? No, I do not. A ***rustic***[6] put a question to me and my mind was a complete blank. I kept ***hammering***[7] at the two sides of the question until I got everything out of it.'‡

* This is the title of a high office. It is not clear who the person referred to was or even from which state he came.

† The identity of the person referred to here is uncertain.

‡ The whole section is exceedingly obscure and the translation is tentative.

Notes

1 otherwise ['ʌðəwaiz] *ad.* 不然，否则

2 sagehood ['seidʒhud] *n.* 圣人

3 menial ['mi:niəl] *a.* 卑贱的

4 Lao 牢，孔子的学生

5 Jack of all trades 杂而不精的人，万事通

6 rustic ['rʌstik] *n.* 乡下人

7 hammer ['hæmə] *v.* 反复推敲；不懈努力

孔子被匡地的人们围困时，他说："周文王死了以后，周代的礼乐文化不都在我这里吗？上天如果想要消灭这种文化，那我也不会掌握它们了；上天如果不消灭这种文化，那么匡人又能把我怎么样呢？"

6. 太宰① 问于子贡曰："夫子圣者与？何其多能也？" 子贡曰："固天纵② 之将圣，又多能也。" 子闻之，曰："太宰知我乎？吾少也贱，故多能鄙事③。君子多乎哉？不多也。"

太宰问子贡说："孔先生是位圣人吧？为什么这样多才多艺呢？" 子贡说："这一定是上天让他成为圣人，而且使他多才多艺。" 孔子听到后说："太宰怎么会了解我呢？我小时候穷苦，所以会许多卑贱的技艺。君子会有这么多的技艺吗？不会的。"

7. 牢④ 曰："子云：'吾不试⑤，故艺。'"

牢说：孔子说过："'我（年轻时）没有去做官，所以学会许多技艺。'"

8. 子曰："吾有知乎哉？无知也。有鄙夫⑥

---

① 太宰：官名，掌握国君宫廷事务。这里的太宰，有人说是吴国的太宰伯，但不能确认。

② 纵：让，使，不加限量。

③ 鄙事：卑贱的事情。

④ 牢：郑玄说此人系孔子的学生，但在《史记 · 仲尼弟子列传》中未见此人。

⑤ 试：用，被任用。

⑥ 鄙夫：孔子称乡下人、社会下层的人。

9. The Master said, 'The ***Phoenix***[1] does not appear nor does the River offer up its ***Chart***[2].* I am done for.'

10. When the Master ***encountered***[3] men who were in mourning or in ceremonial cap and robes or were blind, he would, on seeing them, rise to his feet, even though they were younger than he was, and, on passing them, would ***quicken***[4] his step.†

11. Yen Yüan, ***heaving***[5] a ***sigh***[6], said, 'The more I look up at it the higher it appears. The more I bore into it the harder it becomes. I see it before me. Suddenly it is behind me.

---

* Both the Phoenix and the Chart were auspicious omens. Confuciusis here lamenting the hopelessness of putting the Way into practice in the Empire of his day.

† as a sign of respect.

Notes

1 phoenix [ˈfiːniks] *n.* 凤凰

2 chart [tʃɑːt] *n.* 图表；八卦图

3 encounter [inˈkauntə] *v.* 遇见

4 quicken [ˈkwikən] *v.* 加快

5 heave [hiːv] *v.* 发出

6 sigh [sai] *n.* 叹息

问于我，空空如也①。我叩②其两端③而竭④焉。”

孔子说：“我有知识吗？没有啊。有一个乡下人问我，我对他问的问题本来一点也不知道。我只是从问题的两端去问，这样就把这个问题全部搞清楚了。”

9. 子曰：“凤鸟⑤不至，河不出图⑥，吾已矣夫！”

孔子说：“凤凰不飞来了，黄河中也不出现八卦图了，我这一生恐怕是完了吧！”

10. 子见齐衰⑦者，冕衣裳者⑧与瞽⑨者，见之，虽少，必作⑩；过之，必趋⑪。

孔子遇见居丧的人、当官的人和盲人时，即使他们比自己年轻，也一定要站起来；从他们面前经过时，一定要快步走过以示恭敬。

11. 颜渊喟⑫然叹曰：“仰之弥⑬高，钻⑭之

---

① 空空如也：指孔子自己心中空空无知。

② 叩：叩问、询问。

③ 两端：两头，指正反、始终、上下方面。

④ 竭：穷尽、尽力追究。

⑤ 凤鸟：古代传说中的一种神鸟。传说凤鸟在舜和周文王时代都出现过，它的出现象征着“圣王”将要出世。

⑥ 河不出图：传说在上古伏羲氏时代，黄河中有龙马背负八卦图而出。它的出现也象征着“圣王”将要出世。

⑦ 齐衰：音 zī cuī，丧服，古时用麻布制成。

⑧ 冕衣裳者：指贵族。

⑨ 瞽：音 gǔ，盲。

⑩ 作：站起来，表示敬意。

⑪ 趋：快步走，表示敬意。

⑫ 喟：音 kuì，叹息的样子。

⑬ 弥：更加，越发。

⑭ 钻：钻研。

'The Master is good at leading one on step by step. He ***broadens***[1] me with culture and brings me back to essentials by means of the rites. I cannot give up even if I wanted to, but, having done all I can, it[*] seems to rise sheer above me and I have no way of going after it, however much I may want to.'

12. The Master was seriously ill. Tzu-lu told his disciples to act as ***retainers***[2].[†] During a period when his condition had improved, the Master said, 'Yu has long been practising ***deception***[3]. In ***pretending***[4] that I had retainers when I had none, who would we be deceiving? Would we be deceiving Heaven? Moreover, would I not rather die in your hands, my friends, than in the hands of retainers? And even if I were not given an ***elaborate***[5] funeral, it is not as if I was dying by the ***wayside***[6].'

---

* Throughout this chapter the '*it*' refers to the way of Confucius.

† When Confucius, no longer in office, was not in a position to have them.

Notes

1 broaden [ˈbrɔːdən] *v.* 变宽，使扩大

2 retainer [riˈteinə] *n.* 家臣，侍从

3 deception [diˈsepʃən] *n.* 欺骗

4 pretend [priˈtend] *v.* 假装，伪称

5 elaborate [iˈlæbəreit] *a.* 精心准备的

6 wayside [ˈweisaid] *n.* 路边

弥坚，瞻[①]之在前，忽焉在后。夫子循循然善诱人[②]，博我以文，约我以礼，欲罢不能。即竭吾才，如有所立卓尔[③]。虽欲从之，末由[④]也已。”

颜渊感叹地说：“对于老师的学问与道德，越抬头看，越觉得高；越用力钻研，越觉得深。看着它好像在前面，忽然又像在后面。虽然他的学问这样高深和不容易捉摸，可老师善于有步骤地诱导我们，用各种典籍来丰富我的知识，又用各种礼节来约束我的言行，使我想停止学习都不可能。我尽我所有的才能、力量跟他学习，感觉很成功，好像自己已经能独立站起来了，但要想再向前迈进一步，又不知怎样去做了。”

12. 子疾病，子路使门人为臣[⑤]。病间[⑥]，曰：“久矣哉，由之行诈也。无臣而为有臣。吾谁欺？欺天乎？且予与其死于臣之手也，无宁[⑦]死于二三子之手乎？且予纵不得大葬[⑧]，予死于道路乎？”

---

① 瞻：音 zhān，视、看。

② 循循然善诱人：循循然，有次序地。诱，劝导、引导。

③ 卓尔：高大、超群的样子。

④ 末由：末，无、没有。由，途径，路径。这里是没有办法的意思。

⑤ 为臣：臣，指家臣，总管。孔子当时不是大夫，没有家臣，但子路叫门人充当孔子的家臣，准备由此人负责总管安葬孔子之事。

⑥ 病间：病情减轻。

⑦ 无宁：宁可。“无”是发语词，没有意义。

⑧ 大葬：指大夫之葬。

13. Tzu-kung said, 'If you had a piece of beautiful ***jade***[1] here, would you put it away safely in a box or would you try to sell it for a good price?' The Master said, 'Of course I would sell it. Of course I would sell it. All I am waiting for is the right offer.'

14. The Master wanted to settle amongst the ***Nine Barbarian Tribes***[2] of the east. Someone said, 'But could you put up with their ***uncouth***[3] ways.' The Master said, 'Once a gentleman settles amongst them, what uncouthness will there be?'

Notes

1 jade [dʒeid] *n.* 玉

2 Nine Barbarian Tribes 九夷，中国古代对东方少数民族的统称

3 uncouth [ʌn'ku:θ] *a.* 粗野的，不文明的

孔子病得很厉害，子路便命孔子的学生做家臣，负责料理后事。后来，孔子的病好一些了，就说道：“仲由干这种弄虚作假的勾当居然这么久呀！我本不该有治丧的组织，却一定要派人组织治丧。我骗谁呢？欺骗上天吗？与其在家臣的侍候下死去，我宁可在你们这些学生的侍候下死去，这样不是更好吗？而且即使不能隆重地办理丧葬，难道我就会被丢在路边没人埋吗？”

13. 子贡曰：“有美玉于斯，韫椟① 而藏诸？求善贾② 而沽诸？”子曰：“沽③ 之哉，沽之哉！我待贾者也。”

子贡道：“这里有一块很好的玉，是把它放在匣子里藏起来呢？还是找一个识货的商人卖掉呢？”孔子道：“卖掉吧，卖掉吧！我正在等着识货的人呢。”

14. 子欲居九夷④。或曰：“陋⑤，如之何？”子曰：“君子居之，何陋之有？”

孔子想搬到九夷去住。有人说：“那地方非常落后闭塞、不开化，怎么能住呢？”孔子说：“有君子去住，就不闭塞落后了。”

---

① 韫椟：音 yùn dú，收藏物件的匣子。

② 善贾：识货的商人。

③ 沽：卖出去。

④ 九夷：中国古代对于东方少数民族的通称。

⑤ 陋：鄙野，文化闭塞，不开化。

15. The Master said, 'It was after my return from Wei to Lu that the music was put right, with the ***ya***[1] and the ***sung***[2*] being ***assigned***[3] their proper places.'

16. The Master said, 'To serve high officials when abroad, and my elders when at home, in arranging funerals not to dare to spare myself, and to be able to hold my drink — these are ***trifles***[4] that give me no trouble.'

17. While standing by a river, the Master said, 'What passes away is, perhaps, like this. Day and night it never lets up.'

18. The Master said, 'I have yet to meet the man who is as fond of virtue as he is of beauty in women.'

19. The Master said, 'As in the case of making a ***mound***[5], if, before the very last ***basketful***[6], I stop, then I shall have stopped. As in the case of ***levelling***[7] the ground, if, though ***tipping***[8] only one basketful, I am going forward, then I shall be making progress.'

---

* The *ya* and the *sung* are sections in the *Odes*.

Notes

1 *ya* 《雅》

2 *sung* [sʌŋ] 《颂》

3 assign [ə'sain] *v.* 分配；指定

4 trifle ['traifl] *n.* 琐事，小事

5 mound [maund] *n.* 土墩，小丘

6 basketful ['bɑːskitfəl] *n.* 一篮（的量）

7 level ['levəl] *v.* 弄平

8 tip [tip] *v.* 倾倒

15. 子曰："吾自卫反鲁①，然后乐正②，《雅》、《颂》③各得其所。"

孔子说："我从卫国回到鲁国后，才把乐曲各篇整理出来，使《雅》、《颂》都有合适的安置。"

16. 子曰："出则事公卿，入则事父兄，丧事不敢不勉，不为酒困，何有于我哉。"

孔子说："在外侍奉长官，在家孝敬父兄，有丧事不敢不尽力去办，不被酒食困扰，这些事对我来说有什么困难呢？"

17. 子在川上曰："逝者如斯夫，不舍昼夜。"

孔子在河边，感叹道："消逝的时光就像这河水一样啊，日夜不停地向前流去。"

18. 子曰："吾未见好德如好色者也。"

孔子说："我没有看见过追求道德胜过追求美貌的人。"

19. 子曰："譬如为山，未成一篑④，止，吾止也；譬如平地，虽覆一篑，进，吾往也。"

孔子说："（做学问）好比堆土成山，只要再加一筐土便完成了，但如果这时停下来，那是自己要停止的。又好比在平地上堆山，虽然

① 自卫反鲁：公元前484年（鲁哀公十一年）冬，孔子从卫国返回鲁国，结束了14年游历不定的生活。

② 乐正：调整乐曲的篇章。

③ 雅颂：指雅乐、颂乐等乐曲名称。也指《诗经》中两类不同的诗的名称。

④ 篑：音kuì，土筐。

20. The Master said, 'If anyone can listen to me with ***unflagging***[1] attention, it is Hui, I suppose.'

21. The Master said of Yen Yüan, 'I watched him making progress, but I did not see him realize his ***capacity***[2] to the full. What a pity!'

22. The Master said, 'There are, are there not, young plants that fail to produce ***blossoms***[3], and blossoms that fail to produce fruit?'

23. The Master said, 'It is fitting that we should hold the young in awe. How do we know that the generations to come will not be the equal of the present? Only when a man reaches the age of forty or fifty without distinguishing himself in any way can one say, I suppose, that he does not deserve to be held in ***awe***[4].'

24. The Master said, 'One cannot but give ***assent***[5] to ***exemplary***[6]

只是刚刚倒下一筐土，如果决心努力前进，那还是自己坚持前进的呀！”

20. 子曰：“语之而不惰者，其回也与！”

孔子说：“听我教导而能始终不懈怠的，大概只有颜回一个人吧！”

21. 子谓颜渊曰：“惜乎！吾见其进也，未见其止也。”

孔子谈到颜渊时说道：“可惜（他死了）呀！（在做学问方面）我从来都只看见他不断地进步，没见他停止过。”

22. 子曰：“苗而不秀[①]者有矣夫；秀而不实者有矣夫！”

孔子说：“庄稼出了苗而不吐穗扬花的情况是有的；吐穗扬花而不结果的情况也是有的呀！”

23. 子曰：“后生可畏，焉知来者之不如今也？四十、五十而无闻焉，斯亦不足畏也已。”

孔子说：“年轻人是值得敬畏的，怎么就知道后一代不如前一代呢？如果一个人到了四五十岁时还默默无闻，那他就没有什么值得敬畏的了。”

24. 子曰：“法语之言[②]，能无从乎？改之为

① 秀：稻、麦等庄稼吐穗扬花叫秀。

② 法语之言：法，指礼仪规则。这里指以礼法规则正言规劝。

Notes

1 unflagging [ʌn'flægiŋ] *a.* 不减弱的，不松懈的

2 capacity [kə'pæsiti] *n.* 能力

3 blossom ['blɔsəm] *n.* 花

4 awe [ɔ:] *n.* 敬畏

5 assent [ə'sent] *n.* 同意

6 exemplary [ig'zempləri] *a.* 模范的

words, but what is important is that one should ***rectify***[1] oneself. One cannot but be pleased with ***tactful***[2] words, but what is important is that one should reform oneself. I can do nothing with the man who gives assent but does not rectify himself or the man who is pleased but does not reform himself.'

25. The Master said, 'Make it your guiding ***principle***[3] to do your best for others and to be trustworthy in what you say. Do not accept as friend anyone who is not as good as you. When you make a mistake do not be afraid of ***mending***[4] your ways.'

26. The Master said, 'The Three Armies can be deprived of their ***commanding***[5] officer, but even a common man cannot be deprived of his purpose.'

Notes

1 rectify [ˈrektifai] *v.* 改正

2 tactful [ˈtæktfəl] *a.* 圆滑的；机智的，得体的

3 principle [ˈprinsəpl] *n.* 原则

4 mend [mend] *v.* 改善，纠正

5 commanding [kəˈmændiŋ] *a.* 指挥的

贵。巽与之言①，能无说②乎？绎③之为贵。说而不绎，从而不改，吾末④如之何也已矣。”

孔子说：“用严肃而符合礼法的语言进行规劝，谁能不接受呢？但（只有按它来）改正自己的错误才是可贵的。恭顺赞许的话，谁听了能不高兴呢？但只有认真分析鉴别它（的真伪是非）才是可贵的。只是高兴而不去分析，只是表示听从而不改正错误，这样的人我拿他也没有办法。”

25. 子曰：“主忠信，毋友不如己者，过则勿惮改。”⑤

白话文译文见本书卷一之第 8 段。

26. 子曰：“三军⑥可夺帅也，匹夫⑦不可夺志也。”

孔子说：“一国军队，可以使它丧失主帅；但一个男子汉，却不能强迫他放弃自己的志向。”

---

① 巽与之言：巽，音 xùn，恭顺，谦逊。与，称许，赞许。这里指恭顺赞许的话。

② 说：音 yuè，同“悦”。

③ 绎：原义为“抽丝”，这里指推究，追求，分析，鉴别。

④ 末：没有。

⑤ 此章重出，《学而》篇已有，见本书卷一之第 8 段。

⑥ 三军：12,500 人为一军，三军包括大国所有的军队。此处言其多。

⑦ 匹夫：平民百姓，主要指男子。

27. The Master said, 'If anyone can, while dressed in a ***worn-out***[1] gown ***padded***[2] with old silk ***floss***[3], stand beside a man wearing fox or ***badger***[4] fur without feeling ashamed, it is, I suppose, Yu.

Neither envious nor ***covetous***[5],

How can he be anything but good?'[*]

Thereafter, Tzu-lu constantly recited these verses. The Master commented, 'The way ***summed up***[6] in these verses will hardly enable one to be good.'

28. The Master said, 'Only when the cold season comes is the point brought home that the pine and the ***cypress***[7] are the last to lose their leaves.'

29. The Master said, 'The man of wisdom is never in two minds;[†] the man of benevolence never worries;[‡] the man of courage is never afraid.'

30. The Master said, 'A man good enough as a partner in one's studies need not be good enough as a partner in the ***pursuit***[8] of the Way; a man good enough as a partner in the pursuit of the Way need not be good enough as a partner in a common stand; a man good enough as a partner in a common stand need not be good enough as a partner in the exercise of moral ***discretion***[9].'

---

* Ode 33.

† About right and wrong.

‡ About the future.

27. 子曰："衣① 敝缊袍②，与衣狐貉③ 者立而不耻者，其由也与？'不忮不求④ ，何用不臧？'"子路终身诵之。子曰："是道也，何足以臧？"

孔子说："穿着破旧的丝绵袍子与穿着狐貉皮袍的人站在一起而不认为是羞耻的，大概只有仲由吧。《诗经》上说：'不嫉妒，不贪求，为什么会不好呢？'"子路听了，便反复吟诵这句诗。孔子见了又说："只做到这个样子，怎么能说够好了呢？"

28. 子曰："岁寒，然后知松柏之后凋也。"

孔子说："只有到了寒冷的季节，才知道松树和柏树是最后凋零的。"

29. 子曰："知者不惑，仁者不忧，勇者不惧。"

孔子说："聪明人不会被迷惑，有仁德的人不会忧愁，勇敢的人无所畏惧。"

30. 子曰："可与共学，未可与适道⑤；可与适道，未可与立⑥；可与立，未可与权⑦。"

孔子说："可以一起学习的人，未必可以与他一起追求真理；可以一起追求至真道理的人，

① 衣：穿，当动词用。
② 敝缊袍：敝，坏。缊，音 yùn，旧的丝绵絮。这里指破旧的丝绵袍。
③ 狐貉：用狐和貉的皮做的裘皮衣服。
④ 不忮不求，何用不臧：这两句见《诗经·邶风·雄雉》篇。忮，音 zhì，害的意思。臧，善，好。
⑤ 适道：适，往。这里是志于道，追求道的意思。
⑥ 立：坚持道而不变。
⑦ 权：秤锤。这里引申为权衡轻重。

Notes

1 worn-out *a.* 破旧的
2 pad [pæd] *v.* 填塞，衬填
3 floss [flɔs] *n.* 丝绵絮
4 badger ['bædʒə] *n.* 獾
5 covetous ['kʌvitəs] *a.* 贪图的，贪婪的
6 sum up 计算，总结
7 cypress ['saipris] *n.* 柏树
8 pursuit [pə'sju:t] *n.* 追求
9 discretion [di'skreʃən] *n.* 斟酌的自由；判断力

31. The flowers of the ***cherry***[1] tree,
How they wave about!
It's not that I do not think of you,
But your home is so far away.*

The Master ***commented***[2], 'He did not really think of her. If he did, there is no such thing as being far away.'

* These lines are not to be found in the present *Odes*.

Notes

1 cherry [ˈtʃeri] *n.* 樱桃

2 comment [ˈkɔment] *v.* 评论

未必可以一起坚持真理而不改变；可以一起坚守真理的人，未必可以一起通权达变。”

31.“唐棣① 之华，偏其反而②。岂不尔思，室是远而③。”子曰：“未之思也，夫何远之有？”

古代有一首诗说：“唐棣树的花朵啊，随风翩翩摇摆。怎么会是我不想念你呢？只是由于家住得太遥远了。”孔子说：“他还不是真的想念啊，如果真的想念，又怎么会有什么遥远呢？”

---

① 唐棣：一种植物，属蔷薇科，落叶灌木。

② 偏其反而：形容花摇动的样子。

③ 室是远而：只是住的地方太远了。

Book X

1. In the local community, Confucius was ***submissive***[1] and seemed to be ***inarticulate***[2]. In the ancestral temple and at court, though fluent, he did not speak lightly.

2. At court, when speaking with Counsellors of lower rank he was ***affable***[3]; when speaking with Counsellors of upper rank, he was frank though respectful. In the presence of his lord, his bearing, though respectful, was composed.

卷 十

Notes

1 submissive [səbˈmisiv] *a.* 服从的，恭顺的

2 inarticulate [ˌinɑːˈtikjulit] *a.* 不善于表达的

3 affable [ˈæfəbl] *a.* 友善的

1. 孔子于乡党，恂恂① 如也，似不能言者。其在宗庙、朝廷，便便② 言，唯谨尔。

孔子在本乡的地方上显得很温和恭敬，像是不会说话的样子。但他在宗庙里、朝堂上，却很善于言辞，只是说得比较谨慎而已。

2. 朝，与下大夫言，侃侃③ 如也；与上大夫言，訚訚④ 如也。君在，踧踖⑤ 如也，与与⑥ 如也。

孔子上朝的时候（如果君主还没有到来），他同下大夫说话，是温和而快乐的样子；同上大夫说话，是正直而恭敬的样子。如果君主来了，又是恭敬而心中不安、小心谨慎、威仪适

① 恂恂：音 xù，温和恭顺。

② 便便：辩，善于辞令。

③ 侃侃：说话理直气壮，不卑不亢，温和快乐的样子。

④ 訚訚：音 yín，正直，和颜悦色而又能直言诤辩。

⑤ 踧踖：音 cú jí，恭敬而不安的样子。

⑥ 与与：小心谨慎、威仪适中的样子。

3. When he was summoned by his lord to act as ***usher***[1], his face took on a serious expression and his step became ***brisk***[2]. When he bowed to his ***colleagues***[3], stretching out his hands to the left or to the right, his robes followed his movements without being ***disarranged***[4]. He went forward with quickened steps, as though he was ***gliding***[5] on wings. After the withdrawal of the guest, he invariably reported, The guest has stopped looking back.'

4. On going through the outer gates to his lord's court, he drew himself in, as though the entrance was too small to admit him.

When he stood, he did not occupy the centre of the ***gateway***[6];[*] when he walked, he did not step on the ***threshold***[7].

When he went past the station of his lord, his face took on a serious expression, his step became brisk, and his words seemed more ***laconic***[8].

When he lifted the ***hem***[9] of his robe to ascend the hall, he drew himself in, stopped ***inhaling***[10] as if he had no need to breathe.

When he had come out and ***descended***[11] the first step, relaxing his expression, he seemed no longer to be tense.

When he had reached the bottom of the steps he went forward with quickened steps as though he was gliding on wings.

When he ***resumed***[12] his station, his bearing was respectful.

---

* A position which would have been presumptuous.

Notes

1 usher [ˈʌʃə] *n.* 接待员

2 brisk [brisk] *a.* 轻快的，快的

3 colleague [ˈkɔliːg] *n.* 同事

4 disarrange [ˌdisəˈreindʒ] *v.* 弄乱

5 glide [glaid] *v.* 滑翔

6 gateway [ˈgeitwei] *n.* 入口处，大门

7 threshold [ˈθreʃhəuld] *n.* 门槛

8 laconic [ləˈkɔnik] *a.* 简洁的

9 hem [hem] *n.* 折边，（衣服）下摆

10 inhale [inˈheil] *v.* 吸气

11 descend [diˈsend] *v.* 下来

12 resume [riˈzjuːm] *v.* 重返

中的样子。

3. 君召使摈①，色勃如也②；足躩③如也。揖所与立，左右手，衣前后，襜④如也。趋进，翼如也⑤。宾退，必复命曰："宾不顾矣。"

国君派孔子去接待宾客，孔子的脸色立即矜持庄重，脚步也快起来，他向站在两旁的人行礼，手或向左或向右作揖，衣服前后摆动，却整齐不乱；快步走的时候，像鸟儿舒展开双翅一样。宾客辞别后一定向君主回报说："客人已经不回头张望了。"

4. 入公门，鞠躬如⑥也，如不容。立不中门，行不履阈⑦。过位，色勃如也，足躩如也，其言似不足者。摄齐⑧升堂，鞠躬如也，屏气似不 息者。出，降一等⑨，逞⑩颜色，怡怡如也。没阶⑪，趋进，翼如也。复其位，踧踖如也。

孔子走进朝堂大门，是谨慎而恭敬的样子，就好像没有他的容身之地一样。站的时候绝不站在门的中间，走的时候不踩门坎。当经

① 摈：音 bìn，动词，负责招待国君的官员。

② 色勃如也：脸色立即庄重起来。

③ 足躩：躩，音 jué，脚步快的样子。

④ 襜：音 chān，整齐之貌。

⑤ 翼如也：如鸟儿展翅一样。

⑥ 鞠躬如：谨慎而恭敬的样子。

⑦ 履阈：阈，音 yù，门槛，脚踩门坎。

⑧ 摄齐：齐，音 zī，衣服的下摆。摄，提起。提起衣服的下摆。

⑨ 降一等：从台阶上走下一级。

⑩ 逞：舒展开，松口气。

⑪ 没阶：走完了台阶。

5. When he held the jade ***tablet***[1], he drew himself in as though its weight was too much for him. He held the upper part of the tablet as though he was bowing; he held the lower part of the tablet as though he was ready to hand over a gift. His expression was ***solemn***[2] as though in fear and ***trembling***[3], and his feet were ***constrained***[4] as though following a marked line.

When making a presentation, his expression was ***genial***[5].

At a private audience, he was relaxed.

Notes

1 tablet [ˈtæblit] *n.* 碑；匾

2 solemn [ˈsɔləm] *a.* 庄重的

3 trembling [ˈtrembliŋ] *n.* 发抖，战栗

4 constrained [kənˈstreind] *a.* 勉强的；不自然的

5 genial [ˈdʒiːnjəl] *a.* 亲切的，愉快的

过国君的座位时，面色立刻庄重起来，脚步也加快起来，也没有太多的言辞。提起衣服下摆向堂上走的时候，恭敬谨慎的样子，憋住气好像不呼吸一样。退出来，刚走下一级台阶，脸色便舒展开了，怡然自得的样子。走完了台阶，快快地向前走几步，姿态像鸟儿舒展翅膀。回到自己的位置上时，是恭敬而内心不安的样子。

5. 执圭①，鞠躬如也，如不胜。上如揖，下如授。勃如战色②，足蹜蹜③，如有循④。享礼⑤，有容色。私觌⑥，愉愉如也。

孔子出使到其他诸侯国时，拿着圭，恭敬谨慎，像是举不起来的样子。向上举时好像在作揖，放在下面时好像是在交给别人。脸色庄重得像战栗的样子，步伐也紧凑狭促，好像沿着一条直线往前走。在举行赠送礼物的仪式时，显得和颜悦色。以私人身份和外国君臣会见时，显得轻松愉快。

---

① 圭：一种上圆下方的玉器，举行典礼时，不同身份的人拿着不同的圭。出使邻国，大夫拿着圭作为代表君主的凭信。

② 战色：战战兢兢的样子。

③ 蹜蹜：小步走路的样子。

④ 如有循：循，沿着。好像沿着一条直线往前走一样。

⑤ 享礼：享，献上。指向对方贡献礼物的仪式。使者受到接见后，接着举行献礼仪式。

⑥ 觌：音 dí，会见。

6. The gentleman avoided using dark purple and maroon coloured silk for ***lapels***[1] and ***cuffs***[2]. Red and violet coloured silks were not used for informal dress.

When, in the heat of summer, he wore an unlined robe made of either fine or coarse material, he invariably wore it over an ***underrobe***[3] to set it off.

Under a black jacket, he wore ***lambskin***[4]; under an ***undyed***[5] jacket, he wore ***fawnskin***[6]; under a yellow jacket, he wore fox fur.

His informal fur coat was long but with a short right sleeve.

He invariably had a night robe which was half as long again as he was tall.*

Their fur being thick, ***pelts***[7] of the fox and the badger were used as ***rugs***[8].

Once the period of mourning was over, he placed no restrictions on the kind of ornament that he wore.

Other than skirts for ceremonial occasions, everything else was made up from cut pieces.

Lambskin coats and black caps were not used on visits of ***condolence***[9].

On New Year's Day, he invariably went to court in court dress.

---

* It has been suggested that this sentence has got out of place and should follow the first sentence in the next section.

Notes

1 lapel [lə'pel] *n.* 翻领

2 cuff [kʌf] *n.* 袖口

3 underrobe ['ʌndərəub] *n.* 内衣

4 lambskin ['læmskin] *n.* 小羊皮；羔皮衣

5 undyed [ʌn'daid] *a.* 未染色的，天然色的

6 fawnskin ['fɔ:nskin] *n.* 鹿皮；鹿皮衣

7 pelt [pelt] *n.* 毛皮

8 rug [rʌg] *n.* 小地毯，毛毯

9 condolence [kən'dəuləns] *n.* 哀悼，慰问

6. 君子不以绀緅饰①，红紫不以为亵服②。当暑，袗絺绤③，必表而出之④。缁衣⑤，羔裘⑥；素衣，麑⑦裘；黄衣，狐裘。亵裘长，短右袂⑧。必有寝衣⑨，长一身有半。狐貉之厚以居⑩。去丧，无所不佩。非帷裳⑪，必杀之⑫。羔裘玄冠⑬不以吊⑭。吉月⑮，必服而朝。

君子不用深青透红或黑中透红色的布镶边，不用近乎赤色的浅红色和紫色布来做居家的衣服。夏天穿着粗或细的葛布单衣，但一定着内衣。黑色的衣配黑色的羔羊皮袍，白色的衣配白色的鹿皮袍，黄色的衣配黄色的狐皮袍。平常在家穿的皮袍做得长一些，但右边的袖子

---

① 不以绀緅饰：绀，音 gàn，深青透红，斋戒时服装的颜色。緅，音 zōu，黑中透红，丧服的颜色。这里是说，不以深青透红或黑中透红颜色的布给平常穿的衣服镶上边作饰物。

② 红紫不以为亵服：亵服，平时在家里穿的衣服。古人认为，红紫不是正色，便服不宜用红紫色。

③ 袗絺绤：袗，音 zhěn，单衣。絺，音 chī，细葛布。绤，音 xì，粗葛布。这里是说，穿粗的或细的葛布单衣。

④ 必表而出之：把麻布单衣穿在外面，里面还要衬有内衣。

⑤ 缁衣：黑色的衣服。

⑥ 羔裘：羔皮衣。古代的羔裘都是黑羊皮，毛皮向外。

⑦ 麑：音 ní，小鹿，白色。

⑧ 短右袂：袂，音 mè，袖子。右袖短一点，是为了便于做事。

⑨ 寝衣：睡衣。

⑩ 狐貉之厚以居：狐貉之厚，厚毛的狐貉皮。居，坐。

⑪ 帷裳：上朝和祭祀时穿的礼服，用整幅布制作，不加以裁剪。折叠缝上。

⑫ 必杀之：一定要裁去多余的布。杀，裁。

⑬ 羔裘玄冠：黑色皮礼貌。

⑭ 不以吊：不用于丧事。

⑮ 吉月：每月初一。一说正月初一。

7. In periods of ***purification***[1], he invariably wore a house robe made of the cheaper sort of material.

In periods of purification, he invariably changed to a more ***austere***[2] diet and, when at home, did not sit in his usual place.

8. He did not eat his fill of polished rice, nor did he eat his fill of finely ***minced***[3] meat.

He did not eat rice that had gone sour or fish and meat that had ***spoiled***[4]. He did not eat food that had gone off colour or food that had a bad smell. He did not eat food that was not properly prepared nor did he eat except at the proper times. He did not eat food that had not been properly cut up, nor did he eat unless the proper sauce was available.

Even when there was plenty of meat, he avoided eating more meat than rice.

Only in the case of wine did he not set himself a rigid limit. He simply never drank to the point of becoming confused.

He did not ***consume***[5] wine or dried meat bought from a shop.

Even when he did not have the side dish of ***ginger***[6] cleared from the table, he did not eat more than was proper.

Notes

1 purification [ˌpjuərəfiˈkeiʃən] *n.* 洗净，净化；斋戒

2 austere [ɔsˈtiə] *a.* 朴素的

3 minced [minst] *a.* 切碎的

4 spoil [spɔil] *v.* 腐败，变质

5 consume [kənˈsjuːm] *v.* 吃完，喝光

6 ginger [ˈdʒindʒə] *n.* 姜

要做得短些。睡觉一定有睡衣，而且一定要长过身体。用狐貉的厚皮毛做坐垫。服丧期满以后，什么东西都可以佩带。如果不是礼服，一定要加以剪裁。不穿着黑色的羔羊皮袍和戴着黑色的帽子去吊丧。每月初一，一定穿着朝服去朝拜君主。

7. 齐①，必有明衣②，布。齐必变食③，居必迁坐④。

斋戒沐浴的时候，一定要有布做的浴衣。斋戒的时候，一定要改变平常的饮食，居处也一定要搬移到别处（不与妻妾同房）。

8. 食不厌精，脍⑤不厌细。食饐⑥而餲⑦，鱼馁⑧而肉败，不食。色恶，不食。臭恶，不食。失饪⑨，不食。不时，不食，割不正，不食。不得其酱，不食。肉虽多，不使胜食气⑩。唯酒无量，不及乱⑪。沽酒市脯⑫，不食。不撤姜食，不多食。

---

① 齐：同斋。
② 明衣：斋前沐浴后穿的浴衣。
③ 变食：改变平常的饮食。指不饮酒，不吃葱、蒜等有刺激味的东西。
④ 居必迁坐：指从内室迁到外室居住，不和妻妾同房。
⑤ 脍：音 kuài，切细的鱼、肉。
⑥ 饐：音 yì，陈旧。食物放置时间长了。
⑦ 餲：音 ài，变味了。
⑧ 馁：音 něi，鱼腐烂，这里指鱼不新鲜。
⑨ 饪：烹调制作饭菜。
⑩ 气：同“饩”，音 xì，即粮食。
⑪ 不及乱：乱，指酒醉。不到酒醉时。
⑫ 脯：音 fǔ，熟肉干。

9. After assisting at a sacrifice at his lord's place, he did not keep his ***portion***[1] of the sacrificial meat ***overnight***[2]. In other cases, he did not keep the sacrificial meat for more than three days. Once it was kept beyond three days he no longer ate it.

10. He did not converse at meals; nor did he talk in bed.

11. Even when a meal consisted only of coarse rice and vegetable ***broth***[3], he invariably made an offering from them and invariably did so ***solemnly***[4].

Notes

1 portion [ˈpɔːʃən] *n.* 一份

2 overnight [ˌəuvəˈnait] *ad.* 整夜地

3 broth [brɔːθ] *n.* 汤

4 solemnly [ˈsɔləmli] *ad.* 严肃地

粮食不嫌舂得精，鱼和肉不嫌切得细。粮食霉烂发臭了，鱼和肉腐烂了，都不吃。食物的颜色改变了，不吃。气味变了，不吃。烹调不当，不吃。不是当季的东西，不吃。不是按一定方法切割的肉，不吃。佐料放得不适当，不吃。席上的肉虽多，但吃的量不超过主食。只有酒不限量，但从不喝醉。从市上买来的肉干和酒，不吃。每餐必须有姜，但也不多吃。

9. 祭于公，不宿肉①，祭肉② 不出三日。出三日，不食之矣。

孔子参与国家祭祀典礼时分到的肉，不把它留到第二天。别的祭祀用过的肉留存也都不超过 3 天。超过 3 天，就不吃了。

10. 食不语，寝不言。

吃饭的时候不交谈，睡觉的时候不说话。

11. 虽疏食菜羹③，瓜祭④，必齐⑤ 如也。

即使是糙米饭蔬菜汤，吃饭前也要取出一些来祭祖，而且表情一定恭恭敬敬，就像正式斋戒时那样严肃恭敬。

---

① 不宿肉：不使肉过夜。古代大夫参加国君祭祀以后，可以得到国君赐的祭肉。但祭祀活动一般要持续两三天，所以这些肉就已经不新鲜，不能再过夜了。超过 3 天，就不能再过夜了。

② 祭肉：这是祭祀用的肉。

③ 菜羹：用菜做成的汤。

④ 瓜祭：古人在吃饭前，把席上各种食品分出少许，放在食具之间祭祖。

⑤ 齐：同斋。

12. He did not sit, unless his ***mat***[1] was ***straight***[2].

13. When drinking at a village ***gathering***[3], he left as soon as those carrying ***walking sticks***[4] had left.

14. When the ***villagers***[5] were ***exorcizing***[6] evil spirits, he stood in his court robes on the eastern steps.*

15. When making ***inquiries***[7] after someone in another state, he bowed to the ground twice before sending off the messenger.

16. When ***K'ang Tzu***[8] sent a gift of medicine, [Confucius] bowed his head to the ground before accepting it. However, he said, 'Not knowing its ***properties***[9], I dare not taste it.'

17. The stables caught fire. The Master, on returning from court, asked, 'Was anyone hurt?' He did not ask about the horses.

---

* The place for a host to stand.

Notes

1 mat [mæt] *n.* 草席

2 straight [streit] *a.* 正确的

3 gathering ['gæðəriŋ] *n.* 集会

4 walking stick 手杖

5 villager ['vilədʒə] *n.* 村民

6 exorcize ['eksɔ:saiz] *v.* 驱除

7 inquiry [in'kwaiəri] *n.* 询问，打听

8 K'ang Tzu 康子，季康子

9 property ['prɔpəti] *n.* 特性，性能

12. 席[①] 不正，不坐。

坐席摆放的方法与位置不合礼制，不坐。

13. 乡人饮酒[②]，杖者[③] 出，斯出矣。

行乡饮酒礼的仪式结束后，孔子一定要等老年人都出去了，自己才出去。

14. 乡人傩[④]，朝服而立于阼阶[⑤]。

本地方举行迎神驱鬼的宗教仪式时，孔子总是穿着朝服站在东边的台阶上。

15. 问[⑥] 人于他邦，再拜而送之[⑦]。

孔子托人向在其他诸侯国的朋友问候送礼时，在送行时总要向受托者行两次礼。

16. 康子馈药，拜而受之。曰："丘未达，不敢尝。"

季康子给孔子赠送药品，孔子拜谢之后接受了，却说道："我对药性不很了解，不敢轻易尝试。"

17. 厩焚。子退朝，曰："伤人乎？"不问马。

孔子的马棚失火了。孔子从朝堂回来知道这件事后问道："伤人了吗？"而没有问马的情况。

---

① 席：古代没有椅子和桌子，都坐在铺于地面的席子上。

② 乡人饮酒：指当时的乡饮酒礼。

③ 杖者：拿拐杖的人，指老年人。

④ 傩：音 nuó。古代迎神驱鬼的宗教仪式。

⑤ 阼阶：阼，音 zuò，东面的台阶。主人立在大堂东面的台阶，在这里欢迎客人。

⑥ 问：问候。古代人在问候时往往要致送礼物。

⑦ 再拜而送之：在送别客人时，两次拜别。

18. When his lord gave a gift of cooked food, the first thing he invariably did was to taste it after having ***adjusted***[1] his mat. When his lord gave him a gift of uncooked food, he invariably cooked it and offered it to the ancestors. When his lord gave him a gift of a live animal, he invariably ***reared***[2] it. At the table of his lord, when his lord had made an offering before the meal he invariably started with the rice first.

19. During an illness, when his lord paid him a visit, he would lie with his head to the east, with his court robes draped over him and his grand sash ***trailing***[3] over the side of the bed.

20. When summoned by his lord, he would ***set off***[4] without waiting for horses to be ***yoked***[5] to his carriage.

21. When he went inside the Grand Temple, he asked questions about everything.

22. Whenever a friend died who had no ***kin***[6] to whom his body could be taken, he said, 'Let him be given a funeral from my house.'

23. Even when a gift from a friend was a carriage and horses — since it lacked the ***solemnity***[7] of sacrificial meat — he did not bow to the ground.

Notes

1 adjust [ə'dʒʌst] *v.* 调整

2 rear [riə] *v.* 饲养

3 trail [treil] *v.* 拖带

4 set off 出发

5 yoke [jəuk] *v.* 给…套上轭

6 kin [kin] *n.* 亲戚

7 solemnity [sə'lemniti] *n.* 庄严仪式，庄严，庄重

18. 君赐食，必正席先尝之。君赐腥①，必熟而荐②之。君赐生，必畜之。侍食于君，君祭，先饭。

国君赐给熟食，孔子一定摆正座位先尝一尝。国君赐给生肉，一定煮熟了先给祖宗上供。国君赐给活物，一定要饲养起来。同国君一起吃饭，在国君举行饭前祭礼的时候，一定要先尝一尝。

19. 疾，君视之，东首③，加朝服，拖绅④。

孔子病了，国君来探视，他便头朝东躺着，把上朝的礼服披在身上，系上大带子。

20. 君命召，不俟驾行矣。

国君召见孔子，他不等车马驾好就先步行向前了。

21. 入太庙，每事问。

孔子一进太庙，就问这问那，几乎每一件事他都问到了。

22. 朋友⑤死，无所归，曰："于我殡⑥。"

孔子的朋友死了，没有亲属来负责敛埋，孔子便说：丧事由我来料理吧。

23. 朋友之馈，虽车马，非祭肉，不拜。

朋友的赠品，即使是车马，只要不是祭肉，

---

① 腥：牛肉。

② 荐：供奉。

③ 东首：头朝东。

④ 绅：束在腰间的大带子。

⑤ 朋友：指与孔子志同道合的人。

⑥ 殡：停放灵柩和埋葬都可以叫殡，这里是泛指丧葬事务。

24. When in bed, he did not lie like a ***corpse***[1], nor did he sit in the formal manner of a guest when by himself.

25. When he met a ***bereaved***[2] person in mourning dress, even though it was someone he was on familiar terms with, he invariably ***assumed***[3] a solemn expression. When he met someone wearing a ceremonial cap or someone blind, even though they were well-known to him, he invariably showed them respect.

On passing a person dressed as a mourner he would lean forward with his hands on the ***cross-bar***[4] of his carriage to show respect; he would act in a similar manner towards a person carrying official documents.

When a ***sumptuous***[5] feast was brought on, he invariably assumed a solemn expression and rose to his feet.

When there was a sudden ***clap***[6] of ***thunder***[7] or a violent wind, he invariably assumed a solemn attitude.

孔子在接受的时候都是不行礼的。

24. 寝不尸，居不客。

孔子睡觉时不像死尸一样直躺着，平日家居也不像接见客人或出门做客时一样跪着两膝在席上。

25. 见齐衰[①]者，虽狎[②]，必变。见冕者与瞽者[③]，虽亵[④]，必以貌。凶服[⑤]者式[⑥]之。式负版者[⑦]。有盛馔[⑧]，必变色而作[⑨]。迅雷风烈必变。

孔子看见穿丧服的人，即使是关系很亲密的，也一定改变态度，表示同情。看见当官的和盲人，即使是彼此很熟悉，也一定要有礼貌。在乘车时遇见穿丧服的人，便把身体向前俯，手扶着车前的横木，表示同情。遇见背负国家图籍的人，也这样做以示敬意。做客时，如果有丰盛的菜肴，一定改变神色，站起来致谢。遇见迅雷大风的天气，一定要改变神色以示对上天的敬畏。

---

① 齐衰：zīcuī，指丧服。
② 狎：音 xiá，亲近的意思。
③ 瞽者：盲人，指乐师。
④ 亵：音 xiè，常见、熟悉。
⑤ 凶服：丧服。
⑥ 式：同轼，古代车辆前部的横木。这里作动词用。遇见地位高的人或其他人时，驭手身子向前微俯，伏在横木上，以示尊敬或者同情。这在当时是一种礼节。
⑦ 负版者：背负国家图籍的人。当时无纸，用木版来书写，故称"版"。
⑧ 馔：音 zhuàn，饮食。盛馔，盛大的宴席。
⑨ 作：站起来。

Notes

1 corpse [kɔ:ps] *n.* 尸体
2 bereaved [bi'ri:vd] *a.* 丧失亲人的
3 assume [ə'sju:m] *v.* 呈现；采用
4 cross-bar *n.* 横杆
5 sumptuous ['sʌmptjuəs] *a.* 奢侈的，豪华的
6 clap [klæp] *n.* 霹雳声
7 thunder ['θʌndə] *n.* 雷

26. When climbing into a carriage, he invariably stood squarely and ***grasped***[1] the mounting-cord.

When in the carriage, he did not turn towards the inside, nor did he shout or point.

27. ***Startled***[2], the bird rose up and circled round before ***alighting***[3]. He said, 'The female ***pheasant***[4] on the mountain bridge, how ***timely***[5] her action is, how timely her action is!' Tzu-lu cupped one hand in the other in a gesture of respect towards the bird which, ***flapping***[6] its wings three times, flew away.

Notes

1 grasp [grɑ:sp] *v.* 抓牢

2 startled ['stɑ:tld] *a.* 受惊吓的

3 alight [ə'lait] *v.* 飞落

4 pheasant ['fezənt] *n.* 野鸡

5 timely ['taimli] *a.* 及时的，适时的

6 flap [flæp] *v.* 拍打

26. 升车，必正立，执绥①。车中，不内顾②，不疾言③，不亲指④。

孔子上车时，一定先端正地站好，然后拉着扶手带上车。在车上不回头张望，不高声说话，不用手指指画画。

27. 色斯举矣⑤，翔而后集⑥。曰：“山梁雌雉⑦，时哉时哉！⑧”子路共⑨之，三嗅而作⑩。

孔子在山谷中行走，看见几只野鸡。孔子的脸色一动，野鸡便飞向天空，盘旋一阵，然后又都停在一处。孔子道：“这些山梁上的母野鸡，得到了它们的时运呀，得到了它们的时运呀！”子路向它们拱拱手，它们又振一振翅膀飞走了。

---

① 绥：上车时扶手用的索带。

② 内顾：回头看。

③ 疾言：大声说话。

④ 不亲指：不用自己的手指点。

⑤ 色斯举矣：色，脸色。举，鸟飞起来。

⑥ 翔而后集：飞翔一阵，然后落到树上。鸟群停在树上叫“集”。

⑦ 山梁雌雉：聚集在山梁上的母野鸡。

⑧ 时哉时哉：得其时呀！得其时呀！这是说野鸡时运好，能自由飞翔，自由落下。

⑨ 共：同“拱”。

⑩ 三嗅而作：嗅应为狊字之误。狊，音jù，鸟张开两翅。一本作“戛”字，鸟的长叫声。